Spiritual Caregiving as Secular Sacrament

Practical Theology Series

Editor: John Swinton, School of Divinity and Religious Studies, University of Aberdeen

This new series brings together accessible texts that combine in-depth consideration of theory with suggestions for caring practice. Drawing on the latest research and experience in a range of practice settings, these are informative and thought-provoking resources for practical theologians and practitioners working in health and social care.

other titles in the series

Prayer in Counselling and Psychotherapy
Exploring a Hidden Meaningful Dimension
Peter Madsen Gubi
Foreword by Brian Thorne
ISBN 978 1 84310 519 0

Working Relationships
Spirituality in Human Service and Organisational Life
Neil Pembroke
ISBN 978 1 84310 252 6

Spiritual Dimensions of Pastoral Care
Practical Theology in Multidisciplinary Context
Edited by David Willows and John Swinton
ISBN 978 1 85302 892 2

In Living Colour
An Intercultural Approach to Pastoral Care and Counseling
Second Edition
Emmanuel Y Lartey
ISBN 978 1 84310 750 7

Spirituality and Mental Health Care
Rediscovering a 'Forgotten' Dimension
John Swinton
ISBN 978 1 85302 804 5

Spiritual Caregiving
as Secular Sacrament

A Practical Theology for Professional Caregivers

Ray S. Anderson

Foreword by John Swinton

Jessica Kingsley Publishers
London and Philadelphia

First published in the United Kingdom in 2003
by Jessica Kingsley Publishers
116 Pentonville Road
London N1 9JB, UK
and
400 Market Street, Suite 400
Philadelphia, PA 19106, USA

www.jkp.com

Copyright © 2003 Ray S. Anderson
Printed digitally since 2008

Library of Congress Cataloging in Publication Data
Anderson, Ray Sherman.
    Spiritual caregiving as secular sacrament : a practical theology for
professional caregivers / Ray S. Anderson.
        p. cm.
    Includes bibliographical references and index.
    ISBN 1-84310-746-5 (alk. paper)
        1. Pastoral counseling. 2. Psychotherapy--Religious aspects--Christianity. I. Title.

BV4012.2 .A64 2003
253.5--dc21
                                                                    2002041107

British Library Cataloguing in Publication Data
A CIP catalogue record for this book is available from the British Library

ISBN 978 1 84310 746 0

Contents

Foreword

Ray Anderson loves people. More than that he understands them and knows what it means to care for them in all of their fullness. He not only writes about pastoral care, he lives it. He also understands practical theology. For many people practical theology is nothing more than "handy household hints for ministers": a discipline designed simply to supply the ordained clergy with the necessary knowledge and technology to be efficient ministers. But Ray Anderson's vision is much wider and deeper than that. For Anderson, practical theology is a critical theological discipline that has the potential to offer deep revelation not only to churches and religious communities, but to all people who seek to love, respect and care for one another. And it is in that spirit that, Anderson seeks to open up the spiritual and practical theological dimensions of the caring task. In this book he outlines his passion that all who seek to offer care to other human beings can begin to recognise the importance of the spiritual dimensions of the caring task. Human beings are not simply blobs of flesh, endlessly at the mercy of random, blind natural forces. Rather they are deeply relational beings whose spiritual longings and desires form the very heart of their existence. Only when that spiritual dynamic is recognised and compassionately acknowledged can human beings be seen as meaningful valued creatures with both temporal and transcendent significance.

In this book Anderson provides a model of care which can equip people not only to recognise the significance of the spiritual dimension, but also to be able to develop positive and effective ways of caring for the spirit. This book will be of relevance to people from a wide range of disciplines and offers an important note of clarity to the continuing debate surrounding the role of spirituality within the process of religious, and what Anderson refers to as "secular," caring. I welcome this text as a valuable addition to the field of practical theology – people will be touched, moved and eased into new ways of being and faithful spiritual practice through their encounter with it.

John Swinton,
King's College, Old Aberdeen

Preface

The literature on human spirituality is voluminous and growing, representing versions of New Age spirituality to the recovery of more classical forms of the spiritual disciplines. Mental health caregivers have become increasingly interested in the spiritual dimension of the healing of emotions as well as the body.

Practical theology has not yet provided a significant contribution to this area from the perspective of the basic assumptions which underlie the role and practice of the caregiver in approaching persons as wholistic and spiritual beings. This book is an attempt to fill this gap by offering a theological paradigm of the human person as an ecological construct of physical, spiritual and social being. The spiritual core of a human ecology of living and dying is grounded in social being, not merely in the self as an individual and separated person.

In the chapters that follow I develop a thesis that views all authentic human caregiving as essentially spiritual (whether or not ostensibly religious), and that the *care* given by the caregiver be considered a *sacrament* in a secular (not primarily religious) sense. I want the reader to understand that the word 'spiritual' as used in this book is meant to denote the personal core of the human self apart from whatever religious connotation might be placed on the word. I use the word 'secular' as representing this pre-religious but spiritual reality which constitutes the being of all human persons. Thus, the concept of spiritual caregiving as a secular sacrament also has a pre-religious connotation, though it does not exclude religious belief, rituals and practice as also contributing to caregiving.

If humans are essentially spiritual beings then the mediation of spirituality in the encounter of humans with each other can be considered 'sacramental.' By 'secular sacrament' I thus intend to convey the thought that caregiving is a human encounter which has as its very core an 'open door' to mutual spiritual benefit as well as the mediation of the Spirit of God. The model which I will propose is thus ecumenical in that it intends to serve as a basis for a variety of religious approaches, and is also integrative in that it offers a basis for relating psychological as well as theological insights for the care of persons.

I bring to this project more than 40 years of experience as a pastor, including 25 years of teaching and writing as a practical theologian. It is my hope that this book will make a contribution to the continued development of practical theology as a discipline and professional caregiving as a ministry.

All Scripture references are from *The New Revised Standard Version Bible,* copyright 1989, Division of Christian Education of the National Council of the Churches of Christ in the United States of America.

1

The Spiritual Praxis of Practical Theology

The spiritual dimension of caregiving on the part of religious professionals is often too narrowly focused on edification while, for clinical professionals in the caregiving field, mental health care is often too narrowly focused on overcoming distress, discomfort, or disease. The newly emerging discipline of practical theology offers a paradigm of theological reflection and praxis which provides a more integrative approach by focusing on a more wholistic view of human persons. Pierre Teilhard de Chardin has said that 'We are not human beings having a spiritual experience, but spiritual beings having a human experience' (Gordon McDonald 1994, p.76).

The spirituality of human wholeness

Spirituality lies deeper in the human soul than religious edification. At the same time, spirituality goes further toward human wholeness and well-being than merely the removal of sickness, pain, and distress. Spirituality thus grows out of an integrative matrix which includes both the physical and mental aspects of personal being, grounded in social, personal, sexual, and psychical integration as a praxis of life.

Those who actually practice some form of spiritual ministry have more direct access to the primary subject of theological reflection on human nature than those who deal only with abstract concepts and constructs regarding persons. In the same way, it might be said that a practicing therapist has more direct access to the primary subject of psychological reflection on the self than those who deal only with abstract concepts and constructs regarding persons. Viewed in this way, the discipline of practical theology is methodologically well suited to a dialogue with the practitioners of mental health, as both ground theory in praxis. This is a point which John Swinton (2000a) has made very well in his work on interpersonal relationships and mental health.

The emotional life of the self

At the same time, it must be admitted that, as academic disciplines, the theological study of human persons as well as psychological studies by and large begin with abstract, static, and even impersonal concepts.

One looks in vain through the standard textbooks in systematic theology for a discussion of the emotional life of the self. In the literature on the nature of persons, under the heading of theological anthropology, there is virtually no mention of the subjective aspect of humans as image bearers of God. When one turns to the subject of faith, where the role of emotion might well be expected to contribute to an understanding of the experience of salvation, the focus is on the object of faith rather than the subjective response of the believer. Where faith is taken to be a subjective element of human response, it is treated as a 'gift,' produced by the inward working of the grace of God rather than arising out of the core of the self as a human spiritual act.

Theologians have traditionally displayed an innate disregard for the theological significance of emotion, except to treat it as a relic of the 'old self,' and to use it flagrantly in doctrinal disputes with other theologians! The lack of a theology of emotion in theological literature may be explained by the view of Thomas Oden (1987). Theology, says Oden, has no interest in feelings and emotional responses. The affective life of the self, with its emotions, is better left to the psychologists.

> Christian teaching is not primarily focused upon an analysis of human feelings. However important our emotional responses may be to us, they are not essentially or finally the subject matter of Christian theology, which is a *logos,* a series of reasonings not about one's private feelings but about nothing less than *theos* as known in the faith of the Christian community... Understandably, our dialogue with this incomparable One powerfully affects our feelings...but Christian teaching is less focused on the aftereffects than on the One who elicits and grounds these effects. (p.330)

Duncan Forrester (2000, p.11) cites the fourth-century Cappadocian theologian Gregory of Nyssa as offering this admonition: 'Any action, thought or word which involves passion is out of harmony with Christ and bears the mark of the devil, who makes muddy the pearl of the soul with passions and mars that precious jewel.'

The emotions of God

This dichotomy between faith as an intellectual grasp of *logos*, or the objective Word of God, and the affective elements of faith as experience of self and God, has led to a distortion in our understanding of God as well as to a repression of the subjective life of the self in the faith experience. From the first Christian theologians up to the present time, the doctrine of the impassibility of God has been held with various degrees of emphasis as orthodox theology. That God should have passions and should be affected by anything outside of God's own being was intolerable to the theologians who wanted to preserve the unchangeable and eternally serene character of God. Only recently have theologians begun to question this doctrine and to argue that God indeed experiences pain and suffering as well as pleasure and joy (Wendy Farley 1990; Jürgen Moltmann 1974; Clark Pinnock 2001).

At the same time, this dichotomy forced Christians to repress their feelings for the sake of conformity to the objective 'rule of faith' where right thinking took precedence over contrary feelings. If the affective life of the self is to be studied at all, it was assigned to the growing discipline of psychology, with the assumption that emotions needed to be understood only to be made conformable to the life of faith but added nothing to the quality of that life itself. Thomas Oden (1987), for example, says:

> The empirical inquiry into religious feelings and the emotive life that proceeds from religious experience is a quite different subject area called psychology of religion (an important study, but it is not theology), the study of affective experience that emerges when persons are psychologically and interpersonally impacted by God or by religious symbols and communities (William James, *Varieties of Religious Experience*). (Oden 1987, p.330)

This breach between the disciplines of theology and psychology has its roots in the failure of theology to have a biblical view of God and a failure to construct an integrative model of the human self. In my book *Christians Who Counsel* (Ray Anderson 1990) I attempted just such an integrative model.

Spiritual and mental health

The lack of a coherent and viable vision of the human person as spiritual as well as emotional/mental being plagues the traditional discipline of psychiatric and psychological mental health care. Mental health theorists and practitioners have tended to rely on models which are inclined more toward analytic and individual concepts of the self rather than social and relational constructs. Theoretical models of therapeutic approaches toward healing often lack a pre-theoretical understanding of the nature of human personhood. As a result, effectiveness of a given strategy of providing care can only be measured by judging therapeutic outcomes in accordance with the built-in limitations of the theoretical model being used.

Sigmund Freud (1961), for example, as a representative of classic psychoanalytic theory, considered religious ideation as illusions, 'fulfillments of the oldest, strongest, and most urgent wishes of mankind' (p.39). By ruling out spiritual reality as a component of the self, Freud measured the effectiveness of his therapeutic strategy by assisting his clients in the task of eliminating such illusions as a means of reaching ego maturity. Post-Freudian psychology, it should be noted, has become more open to the reality of religious projection of the self as an authentic expression of the struggle within the ego for a transcendent 'object' with which to identify. Some go further and emphasize the importance of one's belief in God and that God relates to humans in a meaningful way, especially through prayer. For example, Ann and Barry Ulanov (1982, p.36) suggest that

> fantasy becomes an enlarging means of exposure to being. The task is not to get rid of fantasy, which usually results in just making ourselves unconscious of the fantasies that continue anyway below the threshold of awareness. The task is to know our fantasies and disidentify ourselves from them.

The Christian tradition has always understood pastoral ministry to focus on what it called the 'cure of souls' (*cura animarum*) which, according to

Karl Barth (1961b) 'means a concrete actualization of the participation of the one in the particular past, present and future of the other, in his particular burdens and afflictions, but above all in his particular promise and hope in the singularity of his existence as created and sustained by God' (p.885). This rather quaint expression has given way in our time to a more sophisticated technical expression, 'pastoral care.'

Spiritual abuse rather than spiritual healing

To speak of curing rather than of caring can be not only presumptuous but also dangerous. One can all too easily think of some purported cures which have been far more destructive, even demonic, than the original state. Only recently, in the United States, a therapist was found guilty of a crime in the death of a young girl who was being treated by an extreme therapy called 'rebirthing.' As it turned out, the girl suffocated and expired while calling out for help only to have the therapist insist that the procedure continue (*Los Angeles Times* 2001).

Anecdotal stories abound in which attempts to cure mental illness through the exorcism of demons result in tragic consequences, even the death of the person being treated. One such account told of a young woman suffering from mental problems who was suspected of being possessed of a demon. In attempting to exorcize the demon, the woman was beaten with sticks until she was pronounced dead. Those who participated in the exorcism were convinced that they were following biblical principles of dealing with the mentally ill. More recently, the tragic story of Andrea Yates, who drowned her five children in a bathtub, raised the question of demonic oppression and mental illness. Held by the Texas court to be suffering from mental illness she was none the less convicted by a jury and sentenced to life in prison without parole. Her defense was that she was convinced that this was the only way to prevent Satan from destroying her children (*Los Angeles Times* 2002).

In these cases we are reminded of the proverb quoted by Jesus – 'Doctor, cure yourself' (Luke 4:23).

I suspect that as many pastors and spiritual counselors have done damage as psychotherapists. Both professions have their casualties as well as their trophies of healing. What is of concern here is an understanding of the nature of human personhood which can be affirmed by both theologians and health care practitioners as that quality of being and life to which all theories and strategies of care and healing can be accountable. For the most part, one looks in vain for a pre-theoretical understanding of the nature of human personhood underlying even these more promising theories and therapeutic strategies.

A pre-theoretical model

I use the term 'pre-theoretical' in a very specialized sense. In developing theories about why persons behave in certain ways, therapeutic strategies are devised in accordance with these theories. For example, behavior modification therapy is grounded in the theory of a cause and effect relation in human actions. Therefore, if one can modify the cause, one can condition the effect and produce change in behavior. When anecdotal evidence can be found which supports such a theory, it is assumed to be appropriate. By 'pre-theoretical,' I point beyond an explanation of why persons behave in certain ways toward what we may understand as the fundamental nature of human persons.

For example, theoretical physics attempts to explain the behavior of nature as it is observed, assuming some cause and effect relation which accounts for what is observed. Newtonian physics operated on this principle, holding certain assumptions about the fixed relation of time and space. Einstein, along with others, sought to understand the underlying structure of physical particles and came up with what may be called a pre-theoretical assertion as to the fundamental nature of reality. It was the objective nature of reality in its subatomic structure that concerned the new physics, not merely theories which explained the behavior from the perspective of the observer.

It is in this sense that I use the term 'pre-theoretical' to denote the objective nature of human persons lying behind human behavior. All attempts at describing the pre-theoretical are just that – attempts. The point is that each attempt, as with modern physics, must assume that there is an objective reality called 'human personhood' which controls and finally determines the validity of such attempts. The validity of any pre-theoretical model of human nature is to be judged by how useful and viable the pre-theoretical model is in explaining how the various theoretical models work in dealing with human behavior. The pretheoretical model cannot be viewed as just another theory. Nor is the pretheoretical model free to claim theoretical independence. In the end, theories will be judged not by their relation to other theories but by their correspondence to the pre-theoretical model itself – assuming it to be a valid one. Not every physicist agreed with Einstein, but no physicist dares to develop a theory which ignores a pre-theoretical view of reality.

The relation of theory to practice

At the center of the discussion of the nature of practical theology is the issue of the relation of theory to practice. If theory precedes and determines practice, then practice tends to be concerned primarily with methods, techniques and strategies for ministry, lacking theological substance. If practice takes priority over theory, ministry tends to be based on pragmatic results rather than prophetic revelation. A praxis approach does not ignore theory but develops theory in an interactional model with praxis. All good practice includes theory.

Behind the massive work of Karl Barth lies the dynamic interrelation between theory and praxis. The task of theology as Barth construed it is to clarify the presuppositions of church praxis. Praxis comes first precisely because God is 'No fifth wheel on the wagon, but the wheel that drives all wheels.' In his furious response to the Prussian churchman Otto Dibelius, Barth wrote:

> Dibelius characterizes the difference between us as if he was the representation of the Church, i.e. of praxis and love, and I the representative of theology, i.e. of a Christian theory. According to my view any serious undertaking makes that kind of opposition impossible. Praxis and theory, Church and theology, love and knowledge, simply cannot be set over against one another in this kind of abstract way. (Gorringe 1999, p.9)

From the beginning, Barth (1956a) resisted all attempts to portray theory and praxis in opposition to one another. In his early *Church Dogmatics* I/2 he described the distinction between 'theoretical' and 'practical' as a 'primal lie, which has to be resisted in principle' (p.787). The understanding of Christ as the light of life, said Barth (1961b), can be understood only as a 'theory which has its origin and goal in praxis' (p.79).

Praxis is not practice!

At the outset it is necessary to distinguish the concept of 'practice' from 'praxis'. I have discussed this in greater depth in my book *The Soul of Ministry* (1997, pp.25–28). Most of us were taught that truth is discerned as a primary intellectual or mental task. Through abstraction, away from the uncertainty and ambiguity of the experiential world, we are led to believe that reality can be secured with some degree of certainty as 'timeless truths.' Once these truths have been mastered, then one can apply them as a 'practitioner.'

Theological schools quite often divide the curriculum into practical theology and pure theology. By 'practical theology' is often meant the acquiring of skills through experience. In the typical curriculum the truths of the Bible are often taught by scholars who have never served as preachers and teachers in the context of ministry. Other faculty are charged with the task of teaching students how to preach and teach biblical truths by those who have some experience in the practice of ministry.

The praxis of practical theology

The concept of praxis overcomes this dichotomy by linking truth to action. This is the praxis of practical theology, a point more fully developed by James Will (1989).

> But praxis must not be misunderstood as practice. Practice has come to mean the use of external means to attain a theoretically defined end. It suggests that finite and sinful persons may so understand the meaning of God's peace as to be able to devise economic, political, diplomatic, and even military means to attain it. The end of peace is thought to be a transcendent value that appropriate external means may effect. Praxis, on the other hand, is a dialectical process of internally related events from which a result dynamically emerges. Given the finite and ideological character of our preconceptions of peace, they cannot be treated as sufficient definitions of an eternal value to guide our practice. Rather, we need a praxis; that is, peace must be allowed to emerge from a dialogical and dialectical process that may continuously correct our ideological tendencies. Praxis is thus a process of struggle, negotiation, and dialogue toward a genuinely voluntary consensus. (pp.24–25)

Aristotle (1987) once described two quite different ways of viewing an action. The first kind of action he called 'poiesis'. This word denotes an action which produces a result, like a carpenter constructing a cabinet, or a contractor building a house. The end product completes the action regardless of what the future use may be of the product. This future use or purpose, what Aristotle called a 'telos', does not enter into the process of making something (poiesis) (p.182).

For example, a builder might be asked to build a house in accordance with a specific design and blueprint. When the house is finished, the contractor is paid in full if the building has been constructed according to the design. If, after several years, persons living in the house commit illegal or immoral acts, the builder of the house cannot be held liable for these actions. In other words, the ultimate use of the house, or its telos, was not part of the builder's responsibility. This is what Aristotle meant by poiesis. The product completes the action. Figure 1.1 illustrates this kind of action.

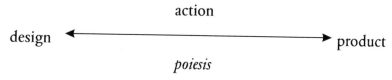

Figure 1.1 Action as poeisis

There is another kind of action, which Aristotle called 'praxis'. While this includes some elements of poiesis, it goes beyond merely producing a product according to a design. With praxis, the telos, or ultimate purpose and value of an action, becomes part of the action. While the design serves to orient the action toward its goal, the ultimate purpose, or telos, informs the action so as to correct the design, if necessary, in order to realize the ultimate purpose. A person involved in praxis, therefore, is not only accountable to implement the design with skill, but to discover the telos through discernment.

In Figure 1.2 the action stands between the design and the telos, with the telos reaching back into the action from the future. The one who performs praxis must have discernment of the ultimate purpose or goal which is becoming evident through the action. It is also the case that only in the process of the action are certain truths concerning the final purpose and goal discovered. The action itself can reveal these truths. This is what

Figure 1.2 Action as praxis

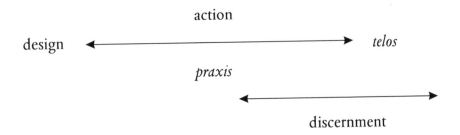

makes *praxis* quite different from practice as the application of truth through a skill or technique. In the process of becoming a person, practice does not always make perfect! It is a process through which one discovers and achieves personhood as a *praxis* through which the ultimate goal is realized as much through transformation as through formation.

On being a person

Becoming a person is not a product which results from the application of theories through parental techniques. Nor is being a person a matter of mastering a set of skills. Rather, personhood is both a gift and an achievement. The praxis of personhood is more of an art than a science. There are skills to be acquired, to be sure, even as there are techniques to be learned and practiced. The inner core of the self, however, is not an empty canvas on which others sketch our portrait, nor is it a blank page on which life writes our story. The self *is* the artist and the self *is* the storyteller. The world, as Shakespeare once said, is our stage and we emerge as actors who are scripting as well as performing our own desires and destiny.

I view the human person as endowed by God with a divine image which serves to promote self-worth, emotional health, and a strong and vital faith in the face of life's inevitable and irrational pain and suffering. The growth of the self requires care, not only self-care but also the care of others such as parents and family members who undertake responsibility for the development of the self through personal and social interactions. Sooner or later, each of us assumes the responsibility for our own self-care which entails, among other things, making wise choices with regard to the persons with whom we live and to whom we look for support, love and community.

Overcoming negative self-esteem

Far too many of us struggle with negative self-esteem and deep wounds to the self which fester and erupt at the most inappropriate moments. I am convinced that this is as much a problem of an inadequate concept of the self as it is with so-called dysfunctional and distorted patterns of behavior. Growth toward wholeness and health requires change as well as transformation.

The psychologist Mary Vander Goot (1987) accurately identifies the source of much unhappiness in contemporary society when she writes:

> Today many people are longing for what now seems like an old-fashioned value, a cause, a goal, or an ideal that could be the lodestar of their lives. The emotional evidence of their predicament is their feeling of fragmentation. Their emotions seem to be like echoes without original sounds. They lack a center: they have no direction. (p.43)

There is a hunger which is necessary for there to be faith. We have all felt it, this longing for fulfillment which lies beyond the horizon of our daily life.

The theologian Emil Brunner (1979) speaks of a 'sorrow-of-heart' which experiences the disharmony of existence without a center which lies outside of the self. To attempt to organize the self around its own center, warns Brunner,

> produces what might be called spiritual or psychological health, but without a center which gives the self a place of hope in God, this 'health' is itself a form of madness, or insanity. To place the central point of existence outside God, who is the true Centre, in the 'I' and the world, is madness; for it cannot be a real centre; the world cannot provide any resting-place for the Self; it only makes it oscillate hither and thither. (p.235)

The Christian psychologist Larry Crabb (1992) suggests that real change must take place from 'the inside out.' 'More often than not,' he suggests, 'psychological efforts do not resolve the deepest issues, which are spiritual... Dealing with our insides can be frustrating. Disciplined Christian living fails to resolve all the problems in our soul' (p.49). I agree. This is why I suggest that effective caregiving comes through a kind of spiritual healing that restores the self to its God-given capacity for faith, hope and love in the context of human relationships. Offering assurance of pardon for sin without restoration of the self is religious malpractice.

Spiritual healing through self-empowerment as a work of God's grace at the deepest core of the self restores in us what sin has destroyed and heals our relationship to God as well as others.

Recovering spiritual health

A physical therapist will require that a patient exercise the muscles in order to facilitate the phases of recovery through the body's own resources for wholeness. Manipulation of body parts does not heal, it only forces the body to function in a way that promotes health. Recovery, in this sense, is a process of going through the phases of growth which lead to the restoration of life at its optimum possibility, given whatever limits and restrictions still apply.

Theologian Jürgen Moltmann (1985) reminds us that health is more than the Utopia of an ideal condition free of all pain and conflicts. Health can be viewed as an objective state of physical, mental, and social well-being. But Moltmann suggests that health may also be viewed as subjective *attitude* on the part of the person.

> Health is then 'the ability to cope with pain, sickness and death autonomously'. To put it more simply: 'Health is not the absence of malfunctionings. Health is the strength to live with them.' In this case, health is not, either, a state of general well-being; it is 'the strength to be human.'

In his criticism of some modern concepts of health, Moltmann goes on to say:

> 'Health' as an ideal of the undisturbed functioning of the physical organs, an existence free of conflict, and a state of general well being, is a utopia, and not a particularly humane utopia at that. It is the utopia of a life without suffering, happiness without pain, and a community without conflicts. Fundamentally speaking it is the ancient utopia of the immortal, eternal life; for only a life of that kind could logically be thought of as a 'state' of well-being like this. (pp.271–2, 273)

Karl Barth (1961a) echoes this theme when he argues that, while sickness is negative in relation to health, it is not necessarily a deterrent to our being human. Health is the strength for human existence, says Barth, 'even those who are seriously ill can will to be healthy without any optimism or illusions regarding their condition.'

> Sickness is obviously negative in relation to health. It is partial impotence to exercise these functions. It hinders man in his exercise of them by burdening, hindering, troubling and threatening him, and causing him pain. But sickness as such is not necessarily impotence to be as man. The strength to be this, so long as one is still alive, can also be the strength and therefore the health of the sick person. And if health is the strength for human existence, even those who are seriously ill can will to be healthy without any optimism or illusions regarding their condition. They, too, are commanded, and it is not too much to ask, that so long as they are alive they should will this, i.e., exercise the power which remains to them, in spite of every obstacle. Hence it seems to be a fundamental demand of the ethics of the sick bed that the sick person should not cease to let himself be addressed, and to address himself, in terms of health and the will which it requires rather than sickness, and above all to see to it that he is in an environment of health. (pp.357–8)

Inevitably, for those with strong religious convictions, the experience of suffering, the pervading presence of evil, and the devastating and tragic losses in life produce a crisis of faith. These are ultimately theological issues and I have attempted to deal with them from the perspective of both a theologian and a pastoral counselor.

Toward a practical theology of *praxis*

What follows in this book is an attempt to develop a practical theology of *praxis* which is based first of all on a pre-theoretical, schematic model of human persons as an integrated gestalt at the personal level. In this model, the spiritual core of human personhood serves as an integrative dynamic of personal, social, physical and mental aspects of the self's journey toward health and wholeness.

In the first few chapters I will lay the foundation for understanding the nature of the human self as a many-faceted system of perceptions, feelings, and self-valuation, all grounded in a network of social relations. Understanding the self as social provides the basis for understanding why dysfunction in social relationships often has such a destructive and crippling effect upon the self.

This pre-theoretical model will then be developed further as a 'real time' process revealing the intrinsic interaction between the physical, spiritual, and social spheres of personal experience. These three spheres constitute an ecological matrix, or structure, with each sphere impinging on and affecting the other in a dynamic process as the person experiences and interacts with the world and with others. Spiritual growth along with emotional/mental growth will then be shown to take place on a 'life continuum' where caregiving involves one's ordinary participation in community as well as extraordinary strategies of intervention and direction. From this model, a profile of spiritual fitness will be developed which takes into account recovery from injuries to the self, living within limitations of disability, and eventually facing and living with the inevitability of death.

To be caregivers is to be committed to the task of seeing and seeking the good of human existence within the context of a community which both supports and sustains human life at its fullest potential. This kind of care was once called the *mutuo consolatio fratrum*. In other words, humanity is to exist fraternally, in mutual consolation, so as to nurture and sustain persons in particular, not merely as a general principle. It is my hope that the chapters which follow will make a contribution to this task.

2

The Integrative Gestalt of the Human Self

For 25 years I have team-taught courses with psychologists in the integration curriculum at our graduate school of psychology. At the very outset I was challenged by a colleague with regard to my use of the terms 'person' and 'personhood' in referring to the self as a proper subject for psychological study. 'In our discipline,' he suggested, 'we can only speak of what we observe as human behavior. To speak of such a thing as "personhood" lying behind personality is only a metaphysical theory and not an empirical reality.'

Because we were both committed to the integration of theological as well as psychological constructs, I argued that personality as applied to God, for instance, is not a proper biblical or theological construct. To say that God is 'one who loves' is a statement about the very being of God, not merely his personality. Karl Barth (1957) argues persuasively that human persons are more than personality as a projection of the self (pp.287–297). In the same way, I suggested, if we are to find a common denominator in our discussion about the human self we must agree that whatever we mean by the term 'personhood,' it must refer to a substance of being lying behind behavior rather than merely a cluster of behavioral attitudes and actions. After all, what is empirical is not just behavior, but that which causes behavior. As I recall, we agreed to disagree. But it was a beginning.

What is human personhood?

While we have come a long way since that time in our discussions, integration between theological and psychological understanding of human persons remains elusive. For the most part, what passes as integration in our curriculum even today seldom goes beyond interdisciplinary discussion. This is a valuable exercise. However, the presumption in such discussions is that each maintains the integrity of his or her particular discipline despite the effort to find ways of linking one discipline to another.

My own approach toward integration, which has led to the writing of this book, is to ask the question, 'What is the nature of the human person as an objective reality which makes a claim upon both theological and psychological concepts and theories as to their validity?' In the training of mental health practitioners as well as with the training of professional religious practitioners, the same question must be asked as a controlling criterion.

Those who view their task as primarily one of promoting spiritual edification as a religious profession must be able to answer the question in such a way that it does not rule out emotional, physical, and mental health as of equal concern to spiritual health. In the same way, those who view their task as primarily one of promoting mental health as professional caregivers must be able to answer the question in such a way that it does not rule out the spiritual dimension of the human self as of equal concern.

The spiritual dimension of personhood

Human persons have an instinctive and existential 'reach' for a transcendent reality, a reality in which one can believe and a reality which integrates the self. But those who turn to forms of spirituality and seek transformation and healing through religious experiences must also come to terms with the reality of human existence at every level.

Those who deny their humanity, or fail to experience it fully, cannot experience their human wholeness, despite fanatical excesses of spirituality. Human life as lived life is integrative living. And it requires integrative competence where both the physical and mental aspects of the self are correlated with the social, personal, sexual, psychical and spiritual.

The discussion of human spirituality has become almost an obsession in our contemporary culture. What is most often lacking in these discussions is a constructive model of human personhood rather than an experiential description of human spirituality. The question needs to be asked again: 'What is the nature of the human person as an objective reality which makes a claim upon both theological and psychological concepts and theories as to their validity?'

The purpose of this chapter

The purpose of this chapter is to provide the first part of an answer to the question from a theological perspective with a view toward the creation of a pre-theoretical model which can be used to validate as well as critically assess the relative merits of theories and strategies for effective mental heath care giving. I am using the term 'pre-theoretical' as an attempt to depict a model of human personhood which goes deeper and lies behind the various psychological and therapeutic theories which deal primarily with attempts to describe and prescribe human behavior. My discussion assumes that there is such an objective reality as 'the self' which both theology and psychology must consider and take into account. Chapters which follow will develop the model more fully, leading to a more fully developed 'gestalt' of human personhood as a working model.

The theory-to-practice issue

In developing my pre-theoretical model of human personhood it will appear that I am departing from the basic method in practical theology by beginning with theory and only later moving to practice. The depiction of the self in this model, however, arises out of my own pastoral counseling experience where those whom I counseled often expressed frustration at their failure to apply biblical principles to their life so as to change their patterns of behavior.

For example, a man whom I will call James came to me for pastoral counsel over repeated episodes of anger which came close to outright hostility and even violence with respect to his wife and children. 'I don't like it when I get angry and lose control of myself,' he confessed. 'I am always ashamed of myself later. But I have to admit that when I am being angry I feel almost a sense of exhilaration, a sense of power, almost as though I were on a drug.' As we discussed his behavior and feelings he expressed frustration at his failure to apply the spiritual principles of self-control and patience. 'I have confessed anger as a sin, I have prayed for forgiveness and a new spirit, but I am the same old angry James.'

As it turned out, James revealed that he had also gone to group therapy under the supervision of a clinical psychologist working specifically on managing one's emotions. He was able to recite some of the basic principles of anger management from a psychological perspective. He had the theory correct, both in terms of his spiritual life with God and his psychological state with himself and others.

James knows that self-control is a virtue; he admires it in others and deplores the lack of it in his own life. As we worked on the deeper issue of shame, it became apparent that what he lacked was not so much the discipline of self-control but a positive and healthy sense of himself as a person of worth and value. 'I don't really know what kind of person I am,' he finally confessed. 'I am one person when I pray to God and another person when I interact with others. Worst of all, I am not a person that I like very well.'

From this experience, as well as many others, I began to see that lying behind the theories of the self and even a theology of the self, is the actual self which demands to be respected, understood, and allowed to exist as the reality that it is, even in a tormented and divided state. We must always go directly to the reality of actual persons rather than to our concept of persons in order to discover the contours of human personhood. Human nature is covered with disgrace and marked by disorder, says theologian Karl Barth (1960a, p.29), but even in our radical depravity there is necessarily hidden our original form.

What follows in this chapter is an attempt to discover this original form, not in some theory but in the actual construct of the self as an integrative *Gestalt* and as a differentiated whole.

The integrative gestalt

This gestalt may be defined as the total configuration or pattern of the lived life. A person's *Gestalt* emerges in the historical process by which a person forms his or her own life pattern in relation to the environment. I am using the term in the broadest sense, not in the technical sense as used by some psychological theorists. Gestalt psychology, pioneered by Frederick (Fritz) and Laura Perls (1976), is based on the German word, *Gestalt*, which is difficult to translate into English. It has the connotation of configuration, structure, theme, or organized whole. I am using the term more in the sense used by the theologian Jürgen Moltmann (1985), who describes the *Gestalt* of a person as:

> the whole human organism – that historical Gestalt which people, body and soul, develop in their environment… In acquiring Gestalt, the person acquires both individuality and sociality; for the Gestalt binds him and his environment into a living unity, and at the same time distinguishes him from that environment as this particular living thing. Gestalt is the form of exchange with the various environments in which a person is identifiable, and with which he can identify himself… Consequently, in the lived Gestalt of a human being, body and soul, the conscious and the unconscious, what is voluntary and what is involuntary, interpenetrate. (pp.159–161)

Steps toward an integrative model

In developing the integrative gestalt several steps need to be taken. First, I will review the biblical use of terms related to the human self as body, soul, spirit, heart, and so on. The inadequacy of using these terms to construct the pre-theoretical model will be shown. Second, I will discuss possible ways of understanding the biblical concept of humans as created in 'the image and likeness of God.' What we will look for are specific qualities which mark off the human person from the non-human while, at the same time, recognizing the fundamental 'creaturely' form of humanity lived in solidarity with all creatures. Finally, I will develop the pre-theoretical model as a basis for creating an integrative gestalt as a practical theology for human health and wholeness.

Surveying the biblical terms relating to the human person

The biblical depiction of the life of the self is hardly analytical and precise. The focus is primarily upon the phenomena of life. The descriptions of the self as related to various components of the person tend to locate the self as the composite function of these elements. What is clear is that the Hebrew view of the person is one of a functional unity rather than a hierarchical duality or even trinity. In my own research and discussion, the relation of body, soul and spirit denotes a unified, yet differentiated, whole rather than a 'tri-partite' view of the self (Anderson 1982, pp.207–214; 1993; 1995a; 1995b).

The Greek word which translates the Hebrew word for soul is *psyche*, from which we have the English word psychology – the study of the soul, or self. The difficulty of attempting to construct a theory of the self upon these terms, however, becomes apparent when we see that the biblical view of the self is a functional composite of both the physical and non-physical life of the person with 'spirit,' or 'breath of life', representing the life and orientation of both soul and body. If we explain the self *essentially*, we say that it is a duality of physical and non-physical life. If we explain the self *functionally*, we say that it appears to have several spheres in which life is experienced and by which the self can be encountered. The soul, the body, and the spirit are spheres of the life of the self. Each of these spheres, however, is expressive of the single life of the self. Here we begin to see the functional unity of the psychological and spiritual spheres of the self as orientations of the life of the self toward the life of others (including God as Spirit) and the life of the self.

When we look at the biblical terms translated into English it quickly becomes apparent that there is little to be gained by attempting to construct a single portrait of human nature based on tracing the English words 'soul,' 'spirit,' 'heart,' and 'body' back to their original language. The most we can say is that it would be wrong to conclude that the biblical terms lead to any kind of dualism between the physical and non-physical dimensions of the person (Anderson 1998, pp.175–194).

The functional nature of biblical terms for the self

The biblical terms *nephesh*, *psyche* (soul) and *ruach*, *pneuma* (spirit) are primarily functional rather than denoting discrete substances or entities. As such, while there are some distinctive patterns of use, the words used by the Bible to denote aspects of human life are not analytical and precise in a philosophical or semantical sense (Boyd 1995, p.155).

THE SOUL

The Hebrew word *nephesh*, translated as 'soul,' is often coupled with other, more concrete words, especially with *basar* (flesh) and *lev, levav* (heart). Biblical Hebrew has no distinct word for 'body' as the Greek does (*soma*).

Nephesh is often used in parallel with *basar* (flesh), never in contrast. The terms are not used as a natural contrast such as 'body and soul,' but often virtually synonymously, being two ways of referring to the self in both its physical and nonphysical existence (Anderson 1982, pp.209–211; Hill 1984, p.100).

While *nephesh* is often used as the equivalent of 'life,' in some cases it refers to the person to whom life is given (Proverbs 3:22). *Nephesh* does not say what a person has, but who the person is who receives life. The fact that *nephesh* can also be used as a pronoun in texts where the word 'life' is also used (Genesis 19:19–20), indicates, as Wolff (1974, p.23) says, 'the "I" is brought out in relief through *nephesh* with its centre in the person, with whose life the Yahwist has been concerned since the definition of Genesis 2:7.'

THE SPIRIT

Ruach (spirit), unlike *basar* (flesh), is never used as a practical synonym for *nephesh*, but is frequently employed in contrast to the *nephesh*. Where *nephesh* means 'life,' *ruach* means 'vigorous life,' or an inspired life. God will often take away the spirit from a person and give another spirit, for better or for worse (1 Samuel 10:6; 16:13, 14). In particular, God will give his own spirit to a chosen person and even be asked to bestow it upon one who seeks it (Psalms 51:10–12).

THE HEART

Heart (*lev*) commonly signifies the seat of intelligence, cunning, good or wicked thoughts, pride, humility, joy, but never compassion, tenderness or intense feeling. The Israelites expressed feeling through terms relating to the bowels, or entrails, not the heart. Consequently, when Jesus rebuked his contemporaries for hardness of heart (Mark 3:5), it is their lack of insight, or sheer stupidity, he referred to, not their callousness and lack of feeling. The heart is the center of the self. It does not constitute a dimension alongside of the body/soul unity of the self, but it is the core of the self as personal being.

Those whom Paul describes as 'fleshly' (*sarkikos*) are also 'soulish' (*psychikos*). Paul never uses the body and the soul as contrasts for spiritual and unspiritual, or for mortal and immortal. Instead, he uses these terms to designate qualities of life expressed through both the physical and nonphysical life. 'Spirit' and 'spiritual' signify a divine quality of life, received as a gift from God and having a share in God's Spirit (1 Corinthians 2:13–3:3). 'Flesh' and 'carnal' do not signify merely a natural or physical quality of life but a corrupt, self-centered and mortal kind of life. It is not human nature that is the enemy of the spirit, but distortion or corruption of that human nature that is the enemy (Hill 1984, pp.101–2).

The life of the person is thus fluid to some extent, as these boundaries of the self expand and shrink, going through changing and shifting commitments. At the same time, the center of the self as the essential person remains constant, even in its growth and change. This accounts for learned personality and behavioral changes with no loss of continuity of the core self.

The image and likeness of God

Human beings, as Thomas Torrance (1981) has said, can be viewed as the 'focal point in the interrelations between God and the universe' (p.129). This 'common ground' of the self's existence as personal, social and spiritual being constitutes what the Bible calls the 'image and likeness of God.' While there are not frequent references to this divine image and likeness in the Bible, the theme is found throughout Scripture (see Psalm 8:5; Hebrews 2:5–9). Humans are of 'more value' than earth creatures (Matthew 6:26; 10:31; 12:9–12; Luke 12:24), and are the object of God's special concern (Hebrews 2:14–18). In this regard, Old Testament theologian W. Eichrodt (1975) says in his reflection on Psalm 8:4, 'Ultimately, therefore it is a spiritual factor which determines the value Man sets upon himself, namely his consciousness of partnership with God, a privilege of which no other creation is considered worthy' (pp.120–1).

The distinctive quality of being human

What distinguishes the human from all other creatures is a spiritual orientation to and personal relation with God as Creator. One way of pointing to this distinctive is to recall that the texts which speak of the 'image and likeness of God' (Genesis 1:26–27; 5:1; 9:6) refer only to humans and not to nonhuman creatures. While it is true that animals also were created as 'living souls' (Genesis 1:20, 21, 24), and there is reference to the 'spirit' (*ruach*) of beasts (Ecclesiastes 3:21), there is no reference in Scripture to animals being created in the divine image and likeness.

I have argued elsewhere that the image and likeness of God (Genesis 1:26–27) can be understood as a capacity for relationship with the self, others and God in a knowing way, and an openness to a future which provides hope and meaning to life (Anderson 1982, pp.215–226; Saucy 1993, pp.17–52).The physical body itself is not held to be in the image of God, such that God has some aspect corresponding to the physical body of humans. None the less, because of the essential unity of body/soul existence, the body is included in the image. Human beings, says Karl Barth (1960a), may be viewed as 'embodied souls' and 'besouled bodies' (pp.350–52). They are in the image of God as upheld by the Spirit of God which attends and summons forth the human spirit.

The relational character of the image

In the second creation account the divine image is not completed in the single individual: 'it is not good that the man should be alone' (Genesis 2:18). Only when the man and the woman exist as complementary forms of human being is there a sense of completeness: 'This at last is bone of my bones and flesh of my flesh;' (Genesis 2:23). From this passage some contemporary theologians view the image and likeness more in relational terms than as a static attribute or rational/spiritual capacity. It is in relationship with other persons as well as with God that the divine image is expressed (Barth 1960a, p.196; Berkouwer 1962, pp.87–90, 179, 197–8). This 'ecological' relation between the physical and the non-physical aspects of the human self, and of one human with another, is positively determined by this divine endowment and is subject to disorder, destructiveness and death when humans fall out of relationship with God through sin.

Openness toward others is part of the fundamental nature of the human self. The self as the expression of the life of the body is an orientation toward the other; thus, the human soul, or self, is not a self-contained entity. The 'individual' is only self-consciously defined in relation to others. Individualism as a philosophy of the human person is a restriction of the self, and can become a distortion of the self.

The self becomes 'singular' in relation with other persons. In other words, our individuality is derived out of relationship. Rather than losing our identity in a relation, we are meant to discover it and have it affirmed. This is a criterion for healthy relationships. Relationships that promote our own sense of selfhood and empower us to be individuals are not only necessary for us to develop a healthy sense of self-identity and self-worth but also a standard by which relationships are to be evaluated and supported. When a relationship becomes oppressive and destructive to the integrity and dignity of the self, the restoration of the individual self is not accomplished by moving out of relationship into sheer individuality, but through finding healing and self-identity in other relationships.

'The individual personal spirit lives solely by virtue of sociality,' wrote Dietrich Bonhoeffer (1998). 'Only in interaction with one another is the spirit of human beings ever revealed; this is the essence of spirit, to be oneself through being in the other' (p.73). Structural openness to other persons, said Bonhoeffer, is not only necessary for the development of one's self-identity but also the basis for our own spiritual identity. Spirituality is thus contingent upon social being as prior to, and the foundation for, religious instincts and experiences.

When the self comes into relation with another, a mutual will is formed which results in a psychic and spiritual unity. The presence of one self to another can be experienced as 'resistance,' with the other forming an opportunity for relation or for opposition. The active will of the other in a relation is a form of resistance which we experience in others, either in a positive or negative form. This resistance provides an objective basis for our own subjectivity, so that our sense of self is based on a practical and not merely theoretical concept. Another way of saying it is that we cannot experience true subjectivity apart from the encounter and relation with other subjects. John Macmurray (1961) says it well: 'I need you to be myself. This need is for a fully positive personal relation in which, because we trust one another, we can think and feel and act together. Only in such a relation can we really be ourselves. If we quarrel, each of us withdraws from the other into himself, and the trust is replaced by fear. We can no longer be ourselves in relation to one another' (p.150).

Macmurray goes on to say that when we are in conflict with one another only reconciliation which restores the original confidence and trust can overcome the negative motivation which results in hostility. Apart from this kind of reconciliation we remain isolated individuals. 'What we really need,' he suggests, 'is to care for one another, and we are only caring for ourselves. We have achieved society, but not community. We have become associates, but not friends' (p.150).

The achievement of community of persons is grounded in actions which embody intentionality to share a common 'soul' or a common history and a common destiny. Macmurray adds: 'The inherent ideal of the personal is a community of persons in which each cares for all the others, and no one cares for himself' (p.159).

The spiritual character of the image

The religious expression of the human soul is based upon the spiritual life of the total human person as a body/soul unity. Spirituality as the essential core of the divine image thus includes the body as well as the soul. True religion, as the Scriptures say, must be grounded in the spiritual integrity of one's relation to the other person as well as to God (see Micah 6:6–8; James 1:27). Humans, as divine image bearers, are 'structurally open' to the Spirit of God as well as other spirits. This means that persons are subject to spiritual violation and spiritual abuse. The Bible witnesses to the destructive effects of coming under the influence of 'unclean spirits,' from the original spiritual seduction of the first humans by Satan (Genesis 3), through the history of the people of Israel, and predominately in the time and ministry of Jesus.

The fact that the entrance of an evil or 'unclean' spirit causes disorientation and disturbance to both body and soul is evidence that the spiritual core of humans lies at the center of the body/soul unity. For example, note some of the typical manifestations of demonic possession described in the New Testament: the healing of the demoniac who was psychologically, socially and physically disturbed and, when healed, was found sitting at the feet of Jesus, fully clothed and in his right mind (Mark 5:20); the healing of the boy who 'threw himself into the fire' when under the control of a demon (Mark 9:14–19). The fact that some of these instances of demonic possession can be explained by either psychological or physical (soul/body) phenomena does not eliminate the possibility that the basic cause may have been due to an evil spirit. We remember that the spiritual core of the person underlies and comes to expression through both body and soul.

A bilingual approach

It is here that a 'bilingual' approach to the healing of persons can be employed, one which can 'listen' to and deal with expressions of pain from both the spiritual as well as the body/soul dimension of the self. Deborah van Duesen Hunsinger (1995) argues convincingly that psychology and theology are quite distinct disciplines which have an asymmetrical relationship. Using the Chalcedonian theological formula concerning the relationship of the humanity and deity of Christ, she holds that the Chalcedon pattern, 'without separation or division' and 'without confusion or change,' offers a theoretical basis for relating psychology and theology in their joint concern for the human person. On the one hand, she views Barth as having the most adequate theology as clearly distinguished from psychology but not excluding genuine scientific exploration of the phenomenon of the human. On the other hand, she views Jung as having the most effective theory of the unconscious drives and archetypes which affect human behavior without impinging upon the proper concerns of theology. The asymmetrical relation gives theology a view of God's precedence (Barth) in defining the true nature of the human, but also allows for the integrity of the discipline of psychology (as with other disciplines) to explore aspects of the human which theology does not explicate. A therapist who can respond to persons as having disturbance in either spiritual or psychological sources is 'bilingual,' by her definition.

Issues of self-identity

While the image of God as the total self must be acknowledged as fully present from the beginning of the human person, the content of this image is only realized through a developmental process. Self-identity, then, is acquired as the particular form of the image of God resulting from the growth and development of the self. The psychological literature on the stages of self and identity development is an expanding and varied field of study. Along with Erik Erikson's (1968; 1982) well-known stages of self-development are Kohlberg's (1973) stages of moral development, Fowler's (1981) stages of faith development, Piaget's (1967) stages of cognitive development, Kohut's (1977) stages of identity formation, and Gilligan's (1982) theory of women's developmental stages. It is not my intention to add to or interact with these developmental theories but to suggest that from a theological perspective, the image of God is developmentally related to the growth of the self as embodied, personal and social being. It is my thesis that the integration of psychological and spiritual aspects of the self can best be seen as part of this developmental trajectory of growth. My focus is on the growth of self-identity based upon the nature of the self as described above.

The social construct of the self

The growth of the person into a self-identity takes place in a context of social and spiritual interaction, with intentionality of love as the motive force. The integration of the various components of the self into an I–Self reality is part of the construct of an I–Thou experience. The mental and physical dimensions of the self are correlated through the openness of the self toward a transcending subject (self).

Martin Buber (1979), the Jewish philosopher most remembered for his classic treatise on the nature of the self as personal and relational, wrote:

> The You encounters me by grace – it cannot be found by seeking. But that I speak the basic word to it is a deed of my whole being, is my essential deed... The basic word I–You can be spoken only with one's whole being. The concentration and fusion into a whole being can never be accomplished by me, can never be accomplished without me. I require a You to become: being I, I say you. (p.62)

The priority of the social relation in the differentiation of the self is a direct implication of the image of God as grounded in co-humanity rather than in individuality. The awakening of the infant to selfhood and the beginning of the development of the image of God as a possibility and personal history of fulfillment is linked to the encounter with others. This begins at the earliest point of the infant's life, and the 'face' that shines upon the infant in love reflects and mediates the love of God, a point articulated eloquently by Hans Urs von Balthasar (1967).

> Through the interdependence of the generations, the social element embraces the individual and influences him... God, who inclined toward his new-born creature with infinite personal love, in order to inspire him with it and to awaken the response to it in him, does in the divine supernatural order something similar to a mother. Out of the strength of her own heart she awakens love in her child in true creative activity... The

essential thing is that the child, awakened thus to love, and already endowed by another's power of love, awakens also to himself and to his true freedom, which is in fact the freedom of loving transcendence of his narrow individuality. No man reaches the core and ground of his own being, becoming free to himself and to all beings, unless love shines on him. (p.87)

Romney Moseley (1991) suggests that there are two factors which enter into self-development:

First, the self is formed as it interacts with the world. Second, there are stages of relative stability as the self progresses from egocentrism to higher levels of social perspective-taking. In the course of development, the self is liberated from its captivity in the egocentric perceptions of early childhood. (p.60)

The ego-self and the social-self

My own formulation of the developmental process is slightly different. Rather than contrasting an egocentric stage with a social stage of self-identity, I see the development of the ego-self as continuous with the development of the social-self.

The newborn infant certainly possesses an ego-self, though largely undeveloped. This ego-self is the seat of feelings (emotions) and the core of what will become self-identity. The infant first of all experiences at a subconscious level a social relation with the primary caregivers through which differentiation at the personal and sexual level gradually emerges. Through this process the full range of psychical feelings and responses are developed from their original limited capacity. The core of the self as spiritual being, which from the beginning has been in place, now is opened up to response to God and to the other. The egocentrism of the self, present from the beginning, is thus developed simultaneously with the self's development of social identity. The process of development is not from egocentric to social perspectival as much as it is from immature self to mature self-identity, both as egocentric and social relating.

In summarizing what has been said about the self from the perspective of biblical anthropology, the following conclusions may be drawn:

- The life of the self is embodied life, with the physical sphere as much a part of the self as the nonphysical (mental) sphere.

- The life of the self is personal life, experienced as openness of spirit to the life of others in a bond of mutual trust and support.

- The life of the self is spiritual life, oriented to God as Spirit and endowed with a value and destiny which has intrinsic worth to God and therefore to all others.

- The image of God represents the totality of the self, as embodied, personal and spiritual life.

- The identity of the self is not so much determined by self-reflection as by intentions and actions through which the self is related to others.

- The development of the self is an integrative process through which the ego-self and the social-self maintain a differentiated and yet unified center of self-identity.

The self as a systemic relationship: a pre-theoretical model

We enter into life as infants held in a social relation to a parenting person or persons. We are not yet differentiated as 'persons' with a self-identity which exists over and against others or even 'it.' Further development entails sexual differentiation with gender identity assimilated into the core self-identity, again with respect to the sexual and personal identity of other persons. The development of psychical experience and capacity comes later, with a deeper capacity to feel and express feelings and emotions.

The growth of the self does not 'add' stages as it develops, but the dimension of the self in each sphere is enlarged and becomes more functional. The psychical life of the infant, for example, is present from birth, and no doubt before. At the same time, the full range of the psychical range of feelings and experiences is quite limited. Children cry when they experience pain, both physically and mentally, but they do not weep out of the depth of sadness of which an adult is capable. Children experience joy and feelings of happiness, but have not yet developed a depth of joy that is able to integrate pain and loss into that joy.

Subsystems of the self

Human persons may be viewed as a set of subsystems, systemically related. That is, each subsystem, with its relative autonomy, which makes up the human person, is part of a whole – which is more than the sum of the parts. One way of understanding the biblical teaching that human persons are created in the 'image and likeness of God' is to think of persons as related simultaneously to God and to each other. To the degree that one system, or one aspect of the human person, operates 'temperamentally,' or idiosyncratically, there is disorder and alienation from the total well-being of the system. The effect of sin is to produce this 'temperament' of individuality, self-aggrandizement, suspicion and fear of the other, and alienation from the shared life with the other and with God.

A pre-theoretical schematic diagram can be constructed which shows the way in which components of the self as an individual and in

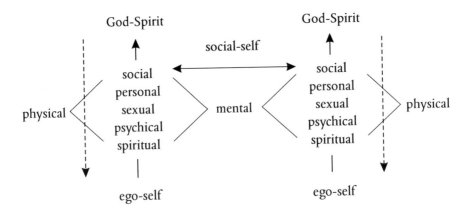

Figure 2.1 Systems of the self

relationship can be viewed. A schematic diagram is somewhat like a wiring diagram for a television or computer. It is not intended to show 'which buttons to push' in order to operate the thing. Rather, it reveals how each 'system' is connected so that if a malfunction occurs a trained technician knows where to locate the problem. Figure 2.1 is just such a 'wiring diagram' for the human person and is meant to be read accordingly. Reading from top to bottom, we see that the progression is from social to personal, to sexual, then psychical and finally spiritual. As spiritual beings, we then have an orientation to God as Spirit which runs right back through each of the other subsets or subsystems of the self. The dotted line represents the growth of the self through each of the spheres, beginning with the social and moving toward the spiritual. The solid line moves from the self through each sphere toward God. This depicts the integration of the self as the self and in relation to the other. The physical and mental aspects of personal life impinge upon each of the spheres and the physical and mental health of each have an effect upon the spheres.

This serves to preserve a balance and positive tension between the physical and mental aspects of the personality for each of the components. If the spiritual dimension should be moved to the side and relate primarily through the mental side of the self, the religious self will become either rationalistic or mystical – both essentially movements away from the concreteness and embodiedness of the self.

In the same way, there are both physical and mental aspects to a healthy psychical and sexual life. And should these become primarily either physical or mental, this will represent a distortion and dysfunction for the self in its process of growth and development.

These system components are not 'stages' through which one passes developmentally in a strict linear fashion. Rather, the model should be viewed more like a spiral staircase, where one continues to make progress developmentally but with each 'rotation' through the process enters into and experiences each 'system' from a more mature (hopefully!) perspective.

The integrative dynamic of the self-system

The developmental model depicted in Figure 2.1 has a twofold dimension. There is a vertical integration of the self as personal being through each of the spheres, with an ego-self identity which includes appropriate mental and physical self-reference. This developmental process requires constant adjustment to the ego-self as changes occur both inwardly and with reference to the embodied life of the self.

At the same time, there is a developmental process where integration of the ego-self with the social-self must take place through the changes which are occurring in this dimension of personal experience. From the standpoint of the self, this integrative project and process is a single one provided that it takes place in a relatively healthy and wholistic way. The depiction of the ego-self and the social-self is schematic and not intended to suggest that the self actually has two centers.

The concept of persons as functioning subsystems, independent and yet essential to the integrity and health of persons has been suggested by Anthony G. Greenwald (1982).

> The usefulness of the concept of self in psychology has been limited by psychologists' attempting to deal simultaneously with the self both as an empirical object of study and as the assumed vehicle of conscious experience. This seems an impossible task... In the multisystem analysis of the person (here labeled personalysis), the self is a subsystem of the person and is partially independent of body, verbal, and social sub-systems. (p.152)

The term 'personalysis' was created by Greenwald and intended to serve parallel to *psycho*analysis to indicate indebtedness to Freud's approach. The elements which comprise the set of subsystems of the self are meant to describe a pre-theoretical or metatheoretical model rather than having well-defined referents. Personalysis thus characterizes the person as a set of subsystems, which Greenwald identifies as body, self, verbal, and social. This differs from Freud's theory of the id, ego, and superego which provided an analysis of the *psyche* (mind) by proposing an analysis of the *person* into subsystems.

Greenwald acknowledges that criticism can be leveled against this personalytic account as unprovable and merely a theory. Indeed, admits Greenwald (1982):

> personalysis has been described here in a fashion that renders it (like psychoanalysis) difficult to disprove... Psychoanalysis orients researchers to look for antecedents and indicators of motivational conflict, and to seek evidence for an active barrier (the agency of repression) that restricts access to knowledge. Personalysis, on the other hand, suggests a search for evidence of independent operation of person subsystems and suggests that important general research tasks for psychologists are to seek and to decipher the codes that define subsystems with the person. (pp.169–170)

Greenwald's four subsystems are not identical with the elements of the subsystem of the self as I have proposed above, but share some interesting similarities. First, both models are built on a more wholistic concept of person, including the physical and mental aspect as well as social dimension. What Greenwald terms 'self' I would call 'spirit' as the essential core of the person with its own 'limited access' and 'language code,' to use his concepts. More significantly, Greenwald supports the methodology of developing a 'pre-theoretical' model of the function of persons in order to aid psychology in developing therapeutic theories and methods. 'Personalysis' comes close to describing an integrative model such as I have presented.

The soul and the self

Charles Gerkin (1984) suggests that the core of the self can be termed the 'soul' in a theological sense, incorporating the various psychological terms.

> To use the designation self is to emphasize the line of experienced continuity and interpretive capacity which emerges from the self's object relations. To use the term ego is to emphasize the coming together of a nexus of forces demanding mediation and compromise... The term *soul* is here used as a theological term that points to the self's central core subject to the ego's conflicting forces and to the ultimate origins of the self in God. The soul is the gift of God bestowed upon the individual with the breath of life. It is thus the self, including its ego conflicts, as seen from an ultimate perspective – the perspective of the self as nurtured and sustained in the life of God. (p.98)

My own use of the term 'self' accords with Gerkin's attempt to speak of a central core of the self as grounded in social differentiation and also including the ego-dynamics subject to psychological assessment and therapeutic attention.

Inadequate integration through the developmental process, however, can lead to a splitting of the ego-self from the social-self, to some degree resulting in some level of dysfunction. In extreme cases, the ego-self may also suffer splitting, which may account for the phenomenon of multiple personality disorder.

From the perspective of a theology of the self as grounded in the image of God, this depiction of the self is intended to show both a developmental process as well as an integrative process as a foundation for further consideration of the healing process which needs to take place where disorder and dysfunction have occurred.

The practical value of the pre-theoretical model

It was statements similar to the one James made in the throes of his frustration that prompted me to begin my study of human personhood: 'I really don't know what kind of person I am.' My attempt in developing the pre-critical model is to get behind theories about human spirituality and mental health to the core of personhood itself. Of necessity, this model, like the wiring diagram of a computer's circuits, appears abstract when viewed apart from the day-to-day life of persons. At the same time, however, as with the paradigms used by physicists, this model directs us toward the objective reality of persons rather than away from them. The differentiated, yet wholistic, structure of the self explains to some degree the failure of spiritual principles to mediate James's anger due to the lack of integration of various subsystems and, particularly, due to the splitting of the spiritual and mental aspect apart from the social and personal spheres. Therapeutic strategies as well as strategies and techniques of spiritual formation will invariably fail unless integrated by the self's own inner cohesion and unity.

What can be called therapeutic gains in a clinical sense are corrections made in the various subsystems of the self which facilitate a positive and creative relation of each system to the other and to an orientation to God and other persons. This opens up a variety of therapeutic strategies to be used depending upon the specific therapeutic gain to be achieved within each subset. For example, behavior modification works well where there are cause and effect mechanisms which contribute to the functioning of a subsystem. Bio-feedback techniques recognize the systemic connection between the physical and psychical subsystem. Psychoanalytic-oriented therapy can uncover factors in identity formation which are repressed. Object relations psychology can provide new therapeutic strategies for persons who lack positive identity formation and continuity.

The integrative gestalt of the human self can thus be depicted as threefold:

1. There is integration as embodied soul, where the self forms a 'gestalt' in which the physical and mental aspects of personhood are connected as a living whole. Dysfunction and disorder at this level may take on psychosomatic forms as well as loss of self-esteem and a sense of despair and doom.

2. There is integration as related to self, where the self and others are differentiated within a unity of being – so as to be spoken of as being 'one flesh' (Genesis 2:24). Dysfunction and disorder at this level may reflect problems both with interpersonal relationships and with self-defeating anxieties and fears.

3. There is integration as spiritual self, where God is the source of the human spirit. Dysfunction and disorder at this level may take the form of preoccupation with guilt and depression, with symptoms manifest through each of the other two areas.

My teaching colleague, who is a psychologist, responded to my presentation of the pre-theoretical model:

> Typical of a theologian, your model is abstract and analytical with no reference to behavior. As a psychologist and therapist, I begin by observing people in the context of their existence in real time. After all, it was you who said that there is a person there behind the behavior. Where is the person?

His point was valid, though he offered no critical response to the model itself. My purpose in offering the pre-theoretical model is not to shift the focus away from concrete, embodied existence in real time. Rather, in somewhat the same way as a physicist who seeks to construct a model which represents the invisible but fully empirical inner structure of an atom, practical theology does the same with regard to the inner dynamics of the phenomenon which we call human life. This is what the pre-theoretical model is meant to do by showing how the spiritual core of the ego-self is part of a dynamic gestalt where the physical and mental aspects of personal being interface and interact with the social, personal, sexual, and psychical components of the self as an integrative whole.

In response to my colleague I went on to present an extension of the pre-theoretical model into real time. As with a television set, one does not need to see the wiring diagram in order to operate the machine. But there is a screen to observe and buttons to push. So it is with the human self. There is a face to observe, motion to watch, and yes, buttons to push! In the next chapter we will put a 'case' on the pre-theoretical model and plug it in.

3

The Ecological Matrix
of the Human Person

The call came from the hospital. 'Pastor, the doctor has just informed us that our mother, Ellen, must have a feeding tube inserted if she is to survive, as she can no longer ingest food by mouth. My two sisters and my dad don't want to do this as they feel that this would be contrary to her own wishes. But I can't agree. Pastor, can you come over and talk with us, we need help.'

I knew the family well. They were members of the church of which I was pastor at the time, and each professed vital Christian faith. I had made several pastoral visits to the mother in the hospital. It was Martin who called me. He was emotionally upset and angry with his siblings for even considering taking their mother home to die by slow starvation. 'To do this is like killing her,' he told me over the telephone. 'I think that we must just keep her alive so that there may be a chance that God could heal her in answer to our prayers.'

At the hospital, in consultation with the doctor, it became clear that Ellen was suffering from incurable cancer and that, at best, even with a feeding tube, she could live only a few months. I learned one other thing. Although she was barely conscious and unable to converse at this point, she had made it quite clear to her husband that the one thing that she did not want was to 'just become a vegetable' tied to a machine. 'If I am to die,' she told him, 'I want to do it with dignity.'

The ecology of human personhood

I now use this case as a basis for discussion with my students, some of whom are preparing for pastoral ministry and others for the practice

46

of psychotherapy from a Christian perspective. What emerges in our discussion is that there are three overlapping spheres demanding mediation and decision. The physical sphere has become predominant with regard to her medical condition. The social sphere has become critical with regard to the family situation. And the spiritual sphere looms in the background, brought to the forefront by her son Martin's appeal for divine intervention.

The creation story

In reflecting on this case as a practical theologian, I look for clues to the biblical story of creation. The inadequacy of doing a word study of the terms used in Scripture which describe the human person has already been shown in the previous chapter. Using the Bible as a dictionary of semantic terms or as an encyclopedia of theological concepts may produce doctoral dissertations but will be of little help in gaining practical wisdom. The Bible is primarily written as a narrative of God's interaction with human beings, from the story of creation through the drama of sin and redemption leading to a final vision of healing and hope.

The book of Genesis describes the creation of the first humans in dramatic narrative form: 'the Lord God formed man from the dust of the ground, and breathed into his nostrils the breath of life; and the man became a living being' (Genesis 2:7). From this account, the formation of humans from the dust of the ground points to the physical sphere in which personal being comes into existence and on which it is dependent for life itself. A second, spiritual sphere of life is indicated by the 'breath of life' which appears to come directly from the divine Creator. Of no other creature is this said in the biblical account. The 'living being' which we call human being is essentially spiritual being.

The narrative does not end here. There is something missing. 'Then the Lord God said, "It is not good that the man should be alone; I will make him a helper as his partner"' (Genesis 2:18). What is lacking cannot be found through any of the other creatures which the Lord brought forth out of the ground (2:19–20). Only when the Lord has fashioned another human alongside of the first (out of the rib!), is there human speech and human life: 'Then the man said, "This at last is bone of my bones and flesh of my flesh; this one shall be called Woman, for out of Man this one was taken"' (2:23). From this account, we can determine a third sphere of human life which is essential to being complete and whole, the social dimension. Only when there are two humans can it be said that it is 'good' (Anderson 1990, pp.19–20).

These three – physical, social, spiritual – seem to constitute all of the possibilities in describing humans. Each sphere represents what I will call an ecological matrix in which humans exist. I use the term 'ecological' to indicate that the three spheres, while each has its own unique content, interface with each other so as to affect the condition of each.

Obviously the physical sphere includes the brain and whatever mental processes emerge out of cerebral activity, including emotion. The physical sphere also relates humans to the external world (including nonhuman creatures) while the social sphere relates persons to all other humans. The spiritual sphere then includes all that is meant by self-transcendence and openness to the spirit of others, including but not limited to other human persons. I will argue that no other sphere can be suggested equivalent to these three and one could not think of any aspect of human life and existence not included in these three.

The fact that these three spheres are derived from the biblical account of creation is not intended to suggest that knowledge of and access to these three are dependent upon any particular religious conviction. Instead, what is suggested is that any attempt to oppose a secular versus a sacred (religious) view of humanity is overcome by this ecological model. The model which I present is intended to function in a wholistic rather than a partial way. The fact that I have found a theological basis for this model in Scripture does not mean that it cannot be discovered and affirmed as an essential structure of humanity itself.

The case of Ellen

The relevance of this model to the case presented at the beginning of this chapter can now be seen. The physical condition of Ellen has produced a crisis in the social sphere of her relation to the family and of the members of the family to each other. By suggesting that divine intervention in answer to prayer be sought rather than suspending medical treatment, Martin focused on the spiritual sphere as a way of avoiding what appeared to be an inevitable and unacceptable outcome in the physical sphere. I realize that some families in the same situation might disregard the spiritual sphere and attempt to mediate the situation through only the physical and social spheres. At the same time, many of those who provide mental as well as physical health care are becoming increasingly aware of the significance of the role of prayer and other spiritual resources in just such situations.

For example, Claudia Wallis (1996) reports:

Some scientists are beginning to look seriously at just what benefits patients may derive from spirituality. To their surprise, they are finding plenty of relevant data buried in the medical literature. More than 200 studies that touch on the role of religion have been ferreted out by [Jeffrey] Levin of Eastern Virginia and the late Dr. David Larson, a research psychiatrist formerly at the U.S. National Institutes of Health and more recently at the privately funded International Centre for the Integration of Health and Spirituality. Most of these studies offer evidence that religion is good for one's health.

In the case I have presented I have attempted to translate the pre-theoretical model developed in the previous chapter into a 'real time' depiction of how we observe and come to understand persons in their historical context. The ecological matrix as described above can also be presented schematically as a basis for further discussion.

An ecological model

The concept of ecology in the most general sense simply means the relationship of an organism to its environment, or to a structure of interactive forces which mutually determine both the organism and its environment. In psychology, the term was introduced by Allan Wicker (1979) in *Introduction to Ecological Psychology*. Charles Gerkin (1984) also sees the context of self-development as an ecological relationship.

The quality of the self's interpretation is not simply a product of its own individual effort. The infant and mother (and/or other figures who share the mothering role) together make up a social milieu, an ecology, which shapes a certain cast to the 'I am and you are' situation. The later development of partial independence begins to shift more of the interpretive task onto the developing self. But even into adulthood, the basis for interpretation of the meaning of existence remains fundamentally social. (pp.84–85)

I use the term 'ecology' here in a non-technical sense to describe the interaction of the three spheres of the self in its embodied existence, its existence as spiritual being related to God, and its existence with and for the other person(s). The fundamental ecology of human persons is constituted by fellow humanity, or co-humanity.

In Figure 3.1 the spiritual sphere is placed at the center as a reminder that in the pre-theoretical model the spiritual dimension of the self emerges at the core and is the integrative dynamic for the self in its existence as a duality of physical and nonphysical (mental) experience. In its historical existence, that is, in the self's existence in 'real time', the ego-self is to be understood as the integrative center which is fully present in each of the three spheres and is also dependent upon the three spheres for its existence and well-being.

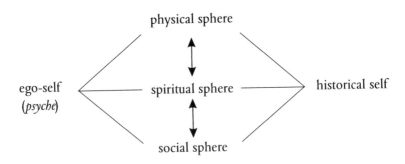

physical sphere

ego-self
(*psyche*)   spiritual sphere   historical self

social sphere

Figure 3.1 The ecological spheres

In the previous chapter I used the term *psyche* to represent the capacity for feelings as distinguished from the personal, social, sexual, and spiritual aspects of the self. Here I am using *psyche* in a broader sense as equivalent to the ego-self, or soul, as the center and source of the life of the person. Thus there is a psychical dimension to the physical, social, and spiritual life of the self as depicted in Figure 3.1. This is to show the ecological relationship between the three spheres of the self as the experienced self in the world and with others.

Applying the model

In Figure 3.1 what I term the historical self is the point at which we encounter each other and where the ego-self comes into expression. In the case described above, Ellen, the mother, is experiencing a devastating and debilitating loss of her physical strength which has already suppressed the expression of her ego-self. The social sphere, represented by her family (and the attending medical staff) are concerned and distressed. At the same time, despite the lack of expression by the ego-self due to the physical deterioration, Ellen is considered to be as much present in a vital sense as when she could talk and express her feelings. We are reminded by those who care for those who appear to be unconscious due to a comatose situation that we should always speak in their presence as though they can hear, even though they cannot respond. This is to reinforce the fact that the ego-self as representative of the personal life of each individual is fully present in each of the three spheres, even though one or more of the spheres may be virtually dysfunctional.

This is what Martin felt so strongly and why he expressed the hope that divine intervention through prayer would reverse the physical deterioration and restore her to a degree of health sufficient to function once again as part of the historical life of the family. As I counseled with him, it became apparent that it was not so much his faith in a miraculous healing which caused him to resist the idea of allowing her to die, but rather his emotional need to hang on to his mother's life even though she was unable to respond to him. I helped him to understand that she was indeed fully present as the person that he loved despite her lack of physical response.

I reinforced the feelings of love which he had for her while leading him to see that the reality of love is also vulnerable to the loss of that which is loved. He had fused his love with the need to protect and preserve her life by any means — finally through the hope that the power of God through prayer would do what neither he nor the doctors could do. It was actually his love for his mother which empowered him to release her to God's power and enter with his family into the sacred space where pain and suffering, even fear of death, can be transformed by divine presence.

The reframing of the relation of love and power by reflecting on the presence of God in human pain and suffering is a way through our powerlessness, rather than our seeking to move away from it, as Arthur

McGill (1982) makes clear. 'As Christians we know how terrible and degrading is the anguish of bodily pain, of social rejection, of the silence of God.' There is something almost demonic about such suffering. At the same time, McGill reminds us, 'They also know that God's grace is moving them toward a world from which the demonic will have completely vanished' (p.116).

As my own father was dying of cancer at our home, our family gathered around him to attend to his final hours. While he was unable to speak, he gave indication that he could hear and understand what we were saying by the movement of his eyes and small gestures with his hands, as if to punctuate sentences which were in his mind but impossible to express with the tongue. Within a few hours, even those responses ceased and he lay motionless, except for an occasional raising of his hand to rub his lower lip, a ritual familiar to us and so common to him that it required no conscious thought. At the end of 36 hours or so there was no response, and the doctor who made a brief visit said that the end was not far away.

It was on a Sunday morning. The Lutheran minister came by following the morning service and walked straight to his bedside. After only a brief greeting to the family he began to recite the 23rd Psalm. 'The Lord is my shepherd, I shall not want. He makes me to lie down in green pastures...' My father, who had not moved a muscle for several hours, suddenly raised his hands and folded them across his chest! Those words, placed in his heart so many years ago, brought forth a response that confirmed for us that God was already beginning to lead him beside the still waters to restore his soul. Here too we experienced the ecological dynamic of the three spheres. Until his last breath he was fully present in the physical, social and spiritual reality of embodied human existence. He died with dignity, as was the expressed wish of Ellen to her own family.

A practical theology of the self

How do we then understand the core of the self as the repository of all that we mean by 'person' and as the essential content of all that we experience as we encounter this person as physical, spiritual and social being? From a psychological perspective, the self can be viewed analytically so as to identify some of the so-called ego dynamics, drives, and conflicts. My focus here is not so much on the psychology of the self as to present a practical theology of the self as a basis for developing strategies of caregiving.

The core of the self can be termed the 'soul' in a theological sense as distinguished from the 'soul' of animals in a more general sense. In a biblical anthropology, both the human and the nonhuman creature possesses a 'soul.' The human soul is the orientation of the total self (Anderson 1982, pp.207–214; 1998, pp.175–194). Charles Gerkin (1984) offers a helpful definition of the soul as 'a theological term that points to the self's central core subject to the ego's conflicting forces and to the ultimate origins of the self in God. The soul is the gift of God bestowed upon the individual with the breath of life. It is thus the self, including its ego conflicts, as seen from an ultimate perspective – the perspective of the self as nurtured and sustained in the life of God' (p.98).

In Figure 3.1, the self is identified as the *psyche*, the Greek word used in the New Testament for soul, or the life of the self. It is used to describe the inner state of Jesus as he contemplates the cross: 'Now is my soul [*psyche*] troubled. And what shall I say? "Father, save me from this hour"? No, for this purpose I have come to this hour' (John 12:27). The deep ambivalence (or 'ego conflicts' as Gerkin describes them) is felt by Jesus in the core of his very being, expressed by the term *psyche*, or soul. This ambivalence was resolved by an intentionality expressed by which the unity of the self (soul) was achieved by integrating the perceived loss at the physical level and at the social level into a behavior that gave meaning to pain, suffering, and loss of life itself, including those relationships which he had developed over the years.

The unity of the self in its threefold ecological existence

Many of the accounts of healing performed by Jesus point to the ecological matrix as described above. For example, Jesus healed a man who had been driven into the wilderness by a 'legion' of demons and was found naked, dragging pieces of chains by which he had been bound. When the people from his own town came out to see what had happened, 'they found the man from whom the demons had gone sitting at the feet of Jesus, clothed and in his right mind' (Luke 8:35). The spiritual life of the man had been abused, he suffered extreme physical distress, and he had been ostracized by his own community. The healing not only restored him to spiritual (mental) sanity and brought comfort to his body but also resulted in his being clothed. Clothing is not only a physical comfort but a symbol of 'being clothed' by others. The miracle of spiritual healing did also clothe the man – he was clothed by his community as a sign of social healing as well. The miracle of healing included the clothing! We often forget that!

On another occasion Jesus was asked to heal a young girl. When he arrived he found that she had apparently died. Taking her by the hand, he raised her up and 'Her spirit returned, and she got up at once. Then he directed them to give her something to eat' (Luke 8:55). The healing of her body restored her spirit, but giving her 'something to eat' restored her life. The miracle of healing included the meal! We often forget that!

Following the mountain-top experience of transfiguration, Jesus returned to his disciples and found them in utter failure over attempts to heal a young boy with epileptic seizures who had been brought by his father. 'Bring your son here,' instructed Jesus. 'While he was coming, the demon dashed him to the ground in convulsions. But Jesus rebuked the unclean spirit, healed the boy, and gave him back to his father' (Luke 9:42). In this case, the diagnosis through the mental/physical sphere led the father to the conclusion that he suffered from epileptic seizures (Matthew 17:14). The healing, however, was attributed to an exorcism of a demon, a spiritual intervention. At the same time, the act of Jesus in 'giving him back to his father' implies a deeper and longer-lasting healing in the restoration of health at the social level. Once again we note that the miracle of healing did not stop with the driving out of the demon (a spiritual healing) nor with the resulting physical relief, but included the social dimension he 'gave him back to his father.' We often forget that!

When Jesus called forth Lazarus from the tomb, he emerged still bound in his grave clothes. The miracle of physical healing, even from death, still left him wrapped, as it were, with his death clothes. 'The dead man came out, his hands and feet bound with strips of cloth, and his face wrapped in a cloth. Jesus said to them, "Unbind him, and let him go"' (John 11:44). In rejoicing over a miracle of healing it is easy to focus on the miracle itself and not realize that the miracle is not concluded by Jesus but by those who 'unbound him' and re-clothed him as a sign of re-entry into life. We often forget that!

In each of these cases, the ecological nature of healing is noted. The overlapping of the three spheres – physical, spiritual, social – produces some ambiguity as to what the source of the problem might be. The removal of the effect of disease and distress is the goal, not the identification of the cause. In many cases, it is true that locating the cause is the most effective way of effecting health and wholeness. The ecological matrix allows for some ambiguity as to the specific cause of a mental/physical health problem as long as the outcome of a therapeutic intervention or strategy of caregiving results in a recovery of function and health as an optimum goal.

Implications for an ecological approach to caregiving

Several conclusions can now be drawn from our discussion of the ecological matrix of the self in the three spheres of its existence.

First, the self (soul) in its totality is present in each of the spheres. If one's life (soul) is reduced to virtually a physical existence, with the loss of social relationships and even loss of spiritual perception of God ('My God, my God, why hast thou forsaken me?'), then the soul, or the selfhood of the person, is fully present up to the point of the spirit's being separated from the body (death). Likewise, the social and spiritual spheres each represent the self in its totality. Yet the nature of the ecological matrix of personhood is such that no single sphere can stand alone as the reality of the self. For example, if a person should go into a coma and be unable to respond at the social or personal level, we would still view the person as a total 'self' rather than merely a physical being. Scientists have demonstrated that the personal development of the infant is linked with the physical bonding that occurs through being held and touched from the very beginning. This is what is meant by the ecological matrix in which the self experiences itself as physical, social, and spiritual.

Second, we must say that any pathology or disorder of the self in one or more of the spheres affects the self in all spheres. This explains why one cannot bless the 'soul' of a person who is hungry without giving that person something to eat. 'If a brother or sister is ill-clad and in lack of daily food, and one of you says to them, "Go in peace, be warmed and filled," without giving them the things needed for the body, what does it profit?' (James 2:15–16). The answer is, of course, it does not profit! If one claims a spiritual relationship with God so that 'God's love abides in him,' but does not provide for the physical needs of a brother or sister and instead 'closes his heart against him,' God's love cannot abide in him (1 John 3:17). In the same way, we could say that to provide for the physical needs of a person and yet deprive him or her of social and spiritual health is to violate the soul or very self of the person. The ecological spheres of the self not only mean that the self is present in each sphere, but that each sphere is essential to some degree to the health and wholeness of the self.

Third, we may say that no authentic approach to the self can bypass the ecological matrix as embodied, social, and spiritual existence. Forms of mental health care which view the self and prescribe therapeutic aid for the self only in terms of the psyche as disembodied, impersonal, and non-spiritual selfhood cannot measure up to a wholistic view of personhood that understands the self (soul) in this threefold way.

Mental health caregivers will be open to the possibility that the source of the problem may be in any of the three spheres and will use therapeutic strategies accordingly. Where disorders appear in human behavior one should not assume that these are always due to spiritual failure, nor should a spiritual source be excluded in every case. To include spiritual openness and health as part of an approach to mental illness should be considered normal and necessary for mental health caregivers.

Fourth, we may say that there will ordinarily be pathologies that are quite specific to each of the three ecological spheres, even though the behavioral symptoms may appear in any of them. For example, a disorder that is essentially biological in origin due to, say, hormonal or chemical imbalance may cause a depression of the self so as to impair function at the social and spiritual levels. One may feel that 'God has abandoned' the self, or that withdrawal from social relationships is the only escape, while the etiology of the problem may be primarily biological rather than spiritual. The ecological nature of the self results in this 'pathological spillover,' with the result that diagnosis becomes more complex than merely observing or noting symptoms.

For caregivers who seek to promote the health of others, there will be openness to the possibility that the presenting problem may be in either of the three spheres and use therapeutic strategies accordingly. Not every disorder or problem of human behavior can be charged to spiritual failure, any more than all problems can be assumed to have a biological cause. At the same time, to include spiritual openness and health as part of the therapeutic goal is not considered a violation of therapeutic and clinical practice for the Christian psychologist or medical doctor. So in addition, a wholistic caregiving approach should be able to discern pathology at the spiritual level of the self and provide appropriate therapy.

Life in relation to others is no protection against abuse, pain and tragic loss. In fact, shared promises and commitments raise the stakes of our losses and griefs. There is something in us that wants to avoid this by withholding commitment and preserving our independence. But solitariness (not solitude!) is a form of abuse for the human spirit. And walking alone provides no certainty of never falling. 'Two are better than one,' wrote the ancient Preacher, 'because they have a good reward for their toil. For if they fall, one will lift up the other; but woe to one who is alone and falls and does not have another to help' (Ecclesiastes 4:9–10).

GROWTH TOWARD HEALTH

Growth toward health is not an individual thing. The self is intrinsically a social reality from which individuality is derived as we experience differentiation in relation to others. Even as an infant experiences selfhood and self-identity through encounter with others the growth and life of the self continues through such interchange. The Apostle Paul was fond of the metaphor of the human body to express the relationships which Christians have as bound together in Christ. 'For just as the body is one and has many members, and all the members of the body, though many, are one body, so it is with Christ' (1 Corinthians 12:12). As each part of the body has its life through the interconnection and interchange with the other parts, so it is with the individual as a member of the community of Christ.

In his letter to the Ephesian church, Paul is even more graphic in using this metaphor to explain the interchange of life necessary to healthy growth and life. 'But speaking the truth in love, we must grow up in every way into him who is the head, into Christ, from whom the whole body, joined and knit together by every ligament with which it is equipped, as each part is working properly, promotes the body's growth in building itself up in love' (Ephesians 4:15–16).

THE EXPERIENCE OF PAIN

The effect of suffering, pain, and experience of loss upon the self is a narrowing one. Anxiety causes the self to tighten up. The flow of blood is restricted. Muscular movements become stiff and constricted. The self retreats into isolation and sets up defenses against the intrusion of further pain. The Latin word for anxiety is *angustia*, a word which means narrowness. The first step toward health is to overcome the effects of this constriction of the self and to emerge into the larger space of self-expression and relation with others. James Leehan (1989) says, 'By overcoming the anxiety (narrowness) imposed upon them, survivors will confront the questions life has presented (an important part of the first movement of the spiritual life), let go of their anger (the forgiveness involved in the second movement), and be freed to receive new life from the God of all life' (p.114).

In her insightful treatment of the inexpressibility of physical pain, Elaine Scarry (1985) reminds us that pain can so narrow the person's social and spiritual horizons that he or she loses a total sense of personal existence. Paradoxically, at the same time, pain fills the entirety of one's existence so that those who seek to enter into that person's existence can only do so through the window of pain. For all other sensations and feelings, there can be found an object and a language by which the feelings can be expressed. Bodily pain is different, Scarry tells us, and tends to isolate and silence the self. Building on this thought, Stanley Hauerwas (1990) says, 'Pain, in effect, is the enemy of community precisely because we cannot feel one another's pain.' Attempts to 'get around' pain by either neutralizing it with pharmaceuticals or seeking to get at the physical source of the pain itself, says Hauerwas, may only 'alienate the patient from his or her own experience' (p.146). Despite this fact, when we do experience pain within a community of support and care, there is an interchange, a transfusion, if you please, so that what life flows out of us flows back into us, filtered through the fabric of intentional care. Within the life of the self in relation to others, there flows the pain of others as well as the joy of others. The move toward health through the creative power of spirit takes place within the life of the body and the care which members have for one another. 'If one member suffers, all suffer with it; if one member is honored, all rejoice together with it' (1 Corinthians 12:26).

My point is this. We must not begin with an abstract concept of the human person where we find it necessary to diagram perfection and imperfection in such a way that their boundaries are precise and unambiguous. When we begin with a view of the self as intended by God to be free of pain and impervious to loss, we end up with a caricature of both God and the human. God is viewed as so abstractly good and powerful that he no longer has a place in a world that is neither. The human self becomes idealized and no longer has any relevance for persons attempting to find their identity in the multiplicity of self-images.

In the face of the pervasive reality of suffering and grieving life's losses, we face two temptations. One is to give way to the inevitability and apparent certainty of suffering by giving up whatever concept of God sustained us in the past. An alternative response is to mask the reality by inventing a coping mechanism of denial, or avoidance, which is really a false hope. Pretending not to see or to feel the evil or pain is a form of self-deception. Temporary relief from the anguish caused by a tragic loss or broken promise by turning to the platitudes and promises of a future hope breaks us off from the real world.

What happened to Ellen?

The case of Ellen and her family with which we began this chapter reminds us that the spiritual sphere must not become a solitary refuge for our own pain and sense of loss. For her son, Martin, the reality of his mother's impending death was too great to bear. It may be that he had not yet dealt realistically with the fact that being physical beings, we are also mortal beings. What was normally a comfortable equation of physical, social and spiritual life in times of health has now split apart and isolated him from the reality of his mother's condition as well as from his siblings and father.

In his grasp for spiritual hope through divine intervention he slipped into the kind of false hope against which Christian Beker (1987), professor of biblical theology at Princeton Seminary, warns when he says:

> When such perceptions of reality become too threatening or are deemed too pessimistic, we create forms of hope which are simply false hope, a result of our unwillingness to see the real world as it is. Thus they are based on the foundation of an illusion. Hope which is nourished by repression, illusion, blindness, or self-deception becomes false hope. Indeed, expectations and hopes which separate themselves from the realities of suffering in our world become demonic hopes; they cast a spell over us and mesmerize us. They are as destructive as the illusory hopes engendered by a drug trip. It is indeed characteristic of the apocalyptic climate of our time that just as the question of suffering numbs us, so the

question of hope is divorced from any meaningful relation to suffering. (p.21)

For additional resources on suffering from a Christian perspective, see Becton (1988), Carson (1990), McGill (1982), Timmer (1988), Towner (1976), and Walsh and Walsh (1985).

What then is my task as a pastoral caregiver in such a situation? First, I must provide a framework or gestalt of understanding by which Martin's emotional pain, perhaps guilt at not being able to sustain his mother in her need, and desperate reach for a divine solution can be disarmed and brought within an ecological context. By meeting him at the level of his own feelings I could assist him into gaining insight into his mother's feelings. Her expressed desire to die with dignity, clearly communicated and accepted by the others, is too threatening for him to grasp. When he is led into what his mother might be feeling, even at this very moment, about her own physical condition, he can re-enter the ecological matrix from which the shock of her impending death has expelled him.

A practical theology of the human condition provides an integrative gestalt in which both realism and hope can be grasped without either denial or delusion. A decision to take Ellen home and attend to her through the painful and, yes, terrible, process of dying will tax the physical, social, and spiritual strength of the caregivers. The fact that this family was finally able to make this decision and carry out this task in a fully human way gave Ellen the dignity that she requested. In such times we discover the dignity and strength of our own humanity in upholding the humanity of another.

4

The Social Ecology
of Human Spirituality

When Ian (not his real name) and his family moved from the east coast to California, they became members of the church of which I was pastor. Ian expressed his concern for the kind of teaching which he expected to find in the church and in my sermons. He wanted to be sure that this would be a church in which he could grow strong in his faith, as he put it, and be firmly grounded in biblical truth. After several months had passed, he came to my office and expressed concern at the way in which my sermons related the biblical text to everyday life, particularly in areas that he considered to be psychological matters and not spiritual truth. 'I don't come to church to hear about my problems or about humanistic theology. I expect to hear sermons which build me up in my faith, not remind me of my problems.'

I told him that I understood what he was expecting. I encouraged him to stay and give us a chance but said that if he and his family could not find the kind of spiritual help and support in our church then I would understand if he turned to another one. In the end, he and his family did stay. But it was only a few months later that I received a telephone call from him. 'Pastor,' he said, 'I need some help. I have just been arrested for indecent exposure.'

As part of his probation he was required to seek counseling from his pastor. As I met with Ian and his wife, I found them composed and outwardly cordial to each other. After a few minutes of casual conversation, I asked, 'Have you talked about the incident when Ian was arrested for indecent exposure?'

'That's between him and God,' she quickly responded. 'He said that he confessed his sin to God and that he had been forgiven. So I have forgiven him too.' I waited for a few moments before speaking. I noted that Ian and his wife were sitting close together on the couch holding hands, but they did not look at each other. Then I asked quietly, 'How do you feel about Ian now?' Letting go of his hand, she began to weep. 'I feel humiliated and angry at what he put our family through. But I know that I'm not supposed to feel that way. I have told him that I forgive him, but he doesn't believe me.'

When I met with Ian and his wife for the next counseling session, Ian spoke up first. 'I can't believe how foolish my behavior was. It was really stupid of me to display myself in public. I'll never understand what came over me, but believe me, I have really learned my lesson. I know better than to do something like that again.' His wife appeared more at peace, and nodded. 'I think that getting caught may be the best thing that happened to Ian,' she said. 'It was painful for all of us, but he has promised not do anything like that again, and I believe him.'

Despite his attempt at taking responsibility for his actions by admitting that they were 'stupid' and stating his intention never to do it again, in subsequent sessions Ian confessed that he had not found the inward peace he sought. Nor was his wife able to sustain her confidence in him. 'I don't really think that he will ever change. He has withdrawn more into himself than ever.' Ian said, 'I think that God has forgiven me, but I cannot forgive myself. I really hate myself for having sexual desires and thoughts that I cannot control.'

Spirituality as an integrated personal life

Looking back at the pre-theoretical model which I discussed in Chapter 1, it is clear that the personal, social and sexual aspects of Ian's ego-self lacked integration. Sexuality had become primarily impersonal, his relationship with his wife lacked intimacy and openness, and spirituality had been split off into a mental construct of doctrine and truth. With respect to the ecological matrix discussed in Chapter 2, his behavior revealed a lack of integration and effective interaction between the physical (sexual), social, and spiritual spheres. Keeping each element of his life in separate compartments became an effective coping mechanism which remained intact as long as he could continue to compartmentalize each sphere. This enabled him to function until he compulsively and impulsively committed a sexual act in public.

When forced to deal with what he had done, he felt shame and resorted to self-condemnation. In an effort to salvage his spiritual identity and repair his coping mechanism he made a private confession of sin to God and claimed God's forgiveness. He also sought his wife's forgiveness, which she felt obliged to grant. When this broke down in the counseling session, he collapsed into self-disgust and self-pity.

Again, using the ecological matrix in order to determine an approach to therapy, we can observe the dichotomy between his spiritual life, which is rooted in a mental construct of true doctrine; his social life, which is based on a superficial involvement in the community of faith; and his marital relationship, which also lacks intimacy and openness at the physical and personal level. Ian lacks effective integration at the personal level, indicating some problems with issues of self-identity and self-esteem. As a result, his spiritual life is rigidly compartmentalized and cognitively objectified.

Issues which emerge

There are several issues which emerge from this case which will become the focus of this chapter. First, I will discuss the concept of spirituality and spiritual formation as essential to an authentic life of faith both in a religious and in a personal sense. What I intend to show is the way in which self-formation at the personal, human level is congruent with spiritual formation as the foundation for authentic and effective faith. Second, the social construct of both spiritual formation and personal growth toward wholeness will be discussed. Here I will show the way in which spirituality is grounded intrinsically in sociality as the precondition and possibility of authentic religious faith. Finally, I will suggest some guidelines by which the life of a community of faith can promote authentic spiritual life and personal growth and the recovery of spirituality for those who have lost it.

The human continuum of spirituality

Contemporary expressions of spirituality can be placed on a continuum with the human spirit as the source of spiritual experience at one end and traditional religious forms of spirituality at the other. The traditional forms of spirituality tend to be individualistic, highly structured and often based on pietistic forms of the classic *imitatio Christi* (imitation of Christ) model. This form of spirituality seeks to 'empty the self' of human propensities for the sake of being filled with the divine impulses of a Christ-like motivation. Examples of writings on classic forms of spirituality are: Thomas à Kempis, *The Imitation of Christ* (1952); Ignatius of Loyola, *The Spiritual Exercises of St. Ignatius* (1992); Thomas Merton, *The Wisdom of the Desert* (1960); Teresa of Avila, *The Interior Castle* (1961). Karl Barth (1956b) comments on such attempts at spiritual being by saying:

> There is nothing, nothing at all, to justify the belief that God has created us for the practice of this self-emptying, or that it has to be recognized and adopted as the way to reconciliation with God. When a man ventures to make this experiment, where does he find himself but in the enclosed circle of his proud being and activity? If faith in its negative form is indeed an emptying, then it is certainly an emptying of all the results of such practices of self-emptying. (p.629)

At the other end of the continuum some are finding new forms of spirituality emerging from the void of secularism and humanism. Matthew Fox (1983), a contemporary Christian theologian and popular author identified with the New Age movement, advocates a form of 'creation spirituality.' He suggests that the persistent teaching of the 'fall/ redemption' motif in traditional theology fails to satisfy the contemporary spiritual seeker.

> A devastating psychological corollary of the fall/redemption tradition is that religion with original sin as its starting point and religion built exclusively around sin and redemption does not teach trust... What if, however, religion was not meant to be built on psychologies of fear but on their opposite – on psychologies of trust and ever-growing expansion of the human person? (p.82)

Marty Kaplan (1996) – a former speechwriter for Vice-President Walter Mondale, Hollywood studio executive, screenwriter and producer described the void of secularism which led to his own 'conversion' to spirituality in this way:

> Harvard, from which I would get a summa in biology, completed my secularization. This is not a criticism. If Harvard had made me a more spiritual person, it would have failed in its promise to socialize me to the values of the educated elite. Those values are secular. The prized act of

mind in the Academy is the laying bare of hidden agendas. The educated person knows that love is really about libido, that power is really about class, that judgment is really about politics, that religion is really about fantasy, that necessity is really about chance. These views come from an Enlightenment that began with Galileo and Newton and a modernity begun by Darwin, Marx and Freud. We are Nietzsche's children, shivering in the pointless void.

When faced with a medical problem which could not be resolved with medication, after reading a book by Deepak Chopra, Kaplan turned to meditation. 'I got more from mind-body medicine than I bargained for. I got religion... The spirituality of it ambushed me.' What Kaplan discovered, however, was not a form of spirituality oriented toward a divine spirit with a name, but an extension of his own spirit through meditation into a cosmic spiritual pantheon. 'The God I have found is common to Moses and Muhammad, to Buddha and Jesus. It is known to every mystic tradition. In mine, it is the Tetragrammaton, the Name so holy that those who know it dare not say it. It is what the Cabala calls Ayin, Nothingness, No-Thingness. It is Spirit, Being, the All.'

My approach will be somewhat different. Rather than a continuum of forms of spirituality I will locate spirituality on the continuum of being human, as created and determined by the God of the Judeo-Christian tradition. From the story of creation to the incarnation of God in the person of Jesus Christ, the form of the human is stamped by the divine image and inspired by the divine Spirit. A practical theology of spirituality begins with a theology of spirituality as a human experience.

Spirituality and our creaturely existence

All creatures bear a common threat to their existence by virtue of being creaturely by nature, created out of the dust of the ground. Creaturely life is suspended in time by the fragile mystery that binds breath to flesh and connects nerve to muscle. But no other creature experiences the double jeopardy of being human. Human existence is never assured by the sustaining of creaturely life by itself. What is a threat to all creatures is also a threat to humans. The non-human creatures have nothing to lose in being no more than their creaturely nature allows them to be. Their nature determines their destiny. But humans have a divinely and spirit-endowed destiny that, while dependent upon survival at the creaturely level, reaches for more than creaturely nature can give. Humans can live out their natural creaturely life and still fail spiritually to become what they are destined to be.

In the biblical account of creation there is a 'solidarity of the sixth day' that binds humans to all creatures through a shared creaturely nature. Both are of the dust of the ground. Humans, however, are destined to share God's life and to enter into the 'seventh day' and experience God's 'rest.' Failure to reach this 'rest' is a failure to reach the essential orientation of human life itself (Hebrews 4:1–13). This is what is meant by saying that humans experience a kind of double jeopardy. They are vulnerable as human creatures to the mortal destiny of all that is creaturely. They are also vulnerable as spiritual beings to the tragic loss of spiritual life and a final destiny to share in the life of God as Spirit.

The spirit of life which determines the creaturely experience of human life is a special orientation of the unity of body and soul. The spirit of life for all other creatures is closed and self-contained. That is, their spirit existence is contained and turned in upon their natural creaturely existence.

The spiritual formation of human life

Human creaturely life, on the other hand, is oriented to a life and spirit beyond that of sheer creaturely existence. It is the body/soul unity of human existence that is spiritual in its orientation and destiny. Humans are not simply beings which also have spirit; they are spiritual beings in the whole of their body/soul existence. This is what distinguishes them from all other creatures as human beings. As Pierre Teilhard de Chardin has said, 'We are not human beings having a spiritual experience, but spiritual beings having a human experience' (McDonald 1994, p.76).

To be human is to exist as a body/soul unity that has a spiritual openness and orientation toward the source of life itself – the Creator Spirit. To be spiritual, therefore, is to exist as a body/soul unity in which knowledge of and relation to the Creator Spirit is experienced in the dual relation of one human to another. In saying this, I am excluding all concepts of spirituality that deny one's own humanity as a body/soul unity or, on the other hand, a spirituality that opposes one's creaturely nature to one's human nature as though these are separate entities. The human person does not have a 'higher' spiritual self and a 'lower' fleshly self; there is no antagonism or dualism which sets spirit over and against the flesh. When the Apostle Paul introduces a distinction between fruit of the spirit and works of the flesh in his ethical admonition, he speaks of nonphysical attitudes and actions as pride, jealousy, and idolatry as 'works of the flesh' (Galatians 5:19–20). Clearly what Paul means by 'flesh' is an introversion of spirit by which one's spirituality becomes a negative rather than positive aspect of one's being.

Since the nature of human life is determined by a spiritual orientation it follows that the development and maturation of personal life is at the same time a process of spiritual formation. The two cannot be separated as isolated functions and tasks. For this reason, spiritual formation as a task belonging to the process of being human is not the implementation of an alien imperative upon otherwise complete human beings. Spiritual formation is not an extracurricular task which attempts to bring persons under some form of religious tutelage. Spiritual formation, properly understood, is intrinsic to the development of the self into the gestalt of human wholeness. What is more, it precedes, and is the essential possibility for, the development of healthy religious spiritual life. 'We should misunderstand the formation of man [sic],' says Dietrich Bonhoeffer (1965), 'if we were to regard it as instruction in the way in which a pious and good life is to be attained' (p.80).

Spiritual formation should no more be understood as merely 'religious education' than as ideological indoctrination. Authentic spiritual formation as both a practice and a goal is neither idealist nor utilitcerian. It is personal, historical, and communal.

Spirituality as a social construct

Because spiritual formation is closely aligned with the task of becoming human and existing in the framework of human relationships, the task of spiritual formation is lodged in the intentionality of community. By intentionality I mean the act of will by which persons enter into commitments toward one another, make promises, and sustain relationship as purposeful and meaningful. We must admit that love is basically intentional rather than merely an affect or attitude. Therefore spiritual formation takes place within the intentionality that lies behind intentions and acts of love. It is the underlying intention, not only the motives of love, which comes to expression in the structure of personhood as constituted in community.

While motives may be located in the individual perceptions of the other in terms of how one views oneself, intentions are located in the structure of relations between persons. In pre-marital counseling with a couple, I always talk about motives and seek to discover underlying attitudes and needs which may enter into the vows which they intend to take. At the marriage service itself, however, I never talk about motives but only intentions. Each is asked directly about their intentions with regard to how love will be expressed toward each other by their actions.

Spirituality, then, is not only bound up in the communal life which cares for and upholds our personal being but also in the same community which holds us accountable to our intentions with regard to the spiritual life and being of others. This seems to be why Scripture is so clear in pointing out that faith in God is measured not by religious actions but by human actions as works of love (James 2:15–17). If a person claims to love God but hate their brothers and sisters, this person is a liar, 'for those who do not love a brother or sister whom they have seen, cannot love God whom they have not seen' (1 John 4:20).

Spirituality is more than religiosity

The spiritual dimension of human personhood constitutes the 'whole' of the self as a psycho-social unity of embodied personal life. Spirituality is to be seen as more than a religious aspect of the self. The spiritual core of the self is what makes religion possible. Spiritual fitness thus is the basis for authentic religious expression as well as for effective mental health. Lack of mental health can be considered to be the result of a partializing or splitting of the self or a lack of spiritual fitness as a wholistic expression of the self in relation to self, others and God.

What Ian lacked in the case with which we began this chapter is what I call spiritual fitness. In splitting off his religious self, as defined by the doctrines which he held as biblical truth, from his human self he became fragile and weak at the core of his being. The coping mechanism by which he survived required immense emotional energy in maintaining the two selves so as to not allow one to compromise or be compromised by the other. Lacking wholeness of personal being he sought holiness as a pseudo-self with God as an objective and impersonal truth.

Wholeness versus holiness

The concepts of wholeness and holiness have been the subject of some discussion in pastoral care literature. Holiness is taken to mean the particular character of a person as the subject of sanctification, as in sanctifying grace applied through the Spirit of God. Wholeness is a more psychological term, tending toward functional well-being. The issue is whether or not one can be in a state of sanctification or grace and, at the same time, lacking in functional wholeness. Those who hold that wholeness produces holiness tend to assume that growth as a function of becoming a whole person is what is meant by the theological term 'sanctification.'

Professor Newton Malony (1983), on the faculty of the Graduate School of Psychology at the Fuller Theological Seminary in Pasadena, California, suggests that the concept of 'whole person' incorporates both psychological wholeness and spiritual holiness. 'To be whole means to be conscious of and adequate in all, not just some of life's environments' (pp.20–21). Seward Hiltner (1983) says that the concept of health includes 'cosmic wholeness,' in which one's life may be in a state of harmony with regard to the whole creation (p.160).

My own view is that wholeness as a psychological state is not a presupposition of holiness as a spiritual state of relatedness to God – good psychological health may not ensure good personal or spiritual health – rather, holiness anticipates and seeks wholeness. I prefer not to set the terms in contrast to each other but rather to view both holiness and wholeness as part of the tension between the actuality and potential of personal being so that one can be making growth in both holiness and wholeness and yet, at the same time, be considered both 'whole' and 'holy' by virtue of being a person created in God's image and the object of God's grace and love. A wholistic approach to mental health thus begins with a positive construct of human personhood rather than merely the absence of sickness. Jürgen Moltmann (1985) says that health may be viewed as 'the ability to cope with pain, sickness, and death autonomously... Health is not the absence of malfunctionings. Health is the strength to live with them... it is the strength to be human' (pp.272–3). Karl Barth (1961a) adds, 'health is the strength for human existence, even those who are seriously ill can will to be healthy without any optimism or illusions regarding their condition' (p.378).

Community versus institution

In a work that is extraordinary in light of his youth and precocious insight, Dietrich Bonhoeffer (1998), at the age of 21 – wrote his doctoral dissertation at the University of Berlin. It was published under the Latin title *Sanctorum Communio* (*Communion of Saints*). In my estimation this dissertation accomplishes what no other work since has achieved in the integration of spirituality, sociality, and human personhood. While his dissertation was ostensibly an attempt to define the nature of the church, he began with a creative and profound examination of the social nature of human personhood as the basis for stating his thesis that Jesus Christ exists in the spiritual structure of human sociality as community (*Gemeinde*) rather than in the institutional form of the church.

'Spirit,' he wrote,

> is necessarily created in community, and the general spirituality of persons is woven into the net of sociality. We will find that all Christian-ethical content as well as all aspects of the human spirit are only real and possible at all through sociality... It will be shown that the whole nature of human spirit [*Geistigkeit*], which necessarily is presupposed by the Christian concept of person and has its unifying point in self-consciousness (of which we will also be speaking in this context), is such that it is only conceivable in sociality. (pp.62, 66)

Because the reality of spirit is first of all a social reality rooted in the nature of human personhood, Bonhoeffer can argue that the social structure of human personhood is intrinsically spiritual. The Spirit of God does not constitute something alongside, or merely inside, a person as an individual. Rather, the Spirit of God joins the human spirit at the core of its social reality. Human spirituality is the core of the self as it becomes a self through social relation with others. Jürgen Moltmann (1985) argues in a similar way when he says,

> The Holy Spirit does not supersede the Spirit of creation but transforms it. The Holy Spirit therefore lays hold of the whole human being, embracing his feelings and his body as well as his soul and reason. He forms the

whole Gestalt of the person anew by making believers 'con-form' to Christ, the first born among many brethren (Romans 8:29). (p.263)

Personal being as structurally open and structurally closed

Bonhoeffer viewed the self as personal being, structurally open to others as well as structurally closed. By this he meant that individuality is derived out of community. Being open to the spirit of other persons awakens and intensifies one's own spirit. Personal being is structurally open and closed. There is no self-consciousness without consciousness of the other, that is, of community.

> God created man and woman directed to one another. God does not desire a history of individual human beings, but the history of the human *community*. However, God does not want a community that absorbs the individual into itself, but a community of *human beings*. In God's eyes, community and individual exist in the same moment and rest in one another. The collective unit and the individual unit have the same structure in God's eyes. (pp.65, 73, 80)

In a passage remarkable for its insight into the paradox of personal relations and personal intimacy he wrote: 'Whereas in experience these acts isolate the I from the You completely, the intimate act is not primarily what constitutes the person as structurally closed. Rather, social intention is inconceivable without corresponding openness. On the other hand, social intention is directed toward the openness of the person, the intimate act toward the person's closedness.' Grounding spirituality in the basic social structure of human being, he added: 'Individual personal spirit lives solely by virtue of sociality, and "social spirit" becomes real only in individual formation; thus genuine sociality itself presses toward personal unity. One cannot speak of the priority of either personal or social being' (p.75).

In our culture we tend to view intimacy as the degree of contact we have with others, primarily achieved through physical proximity and/or verbal communication. Bonhoeffer, however, observed that intimacy is a quality of personal being which is derived out of relation with others. In other words, intimacy is not a means to a relationship but the result, or gift, of the relationship. Bob hoffer wants us to understand that so called intimate acts between persons do not by themselves constitute authentic intimacy. Rather, the openness of one person to another in genuine mutuality creates an intamacy in which the personal being of each is affirmed, respected and valued. In other words, seeking intimacy with another through a physical or even social relationship of touching and proximity is self-defeating. In being genuinely open and in relation with another, we experience personal intimacy as a gift from the other, not in using the other to fulfill the need for intimacy.

The bi-directional nature of human spirituality is represented by the two great commandments first stated in the Old Testament and then reiterated by Jesus: "'You shall love the Lord your God with all your heart, and with all your soul, and with all your mind.' This is the greatest and first commandment. And a second is like it: 'You shall love your neighbor as yourself'" (Matthew 22:38–39; Deuteronomy 6:5; Leviticus 19:18).

Social spirituality and the image of God

As originally created by God, social spirituality reflects the divine image and likeness constitutive of human personhood. The second creation account (Genesis 2) recasts the creation of the human as though only a solitary individual is present. Despite an obvious relation between Adam and God, the divine verdict is that it is not good for the man to be alone. With the creation of the woman, humans are differentiated and yet bound together as male and female, as social beings. The implication is that the divine image spoken of in Genesis 1:26–27 can only be complete as a social construct of personal relation.

Even as the individual self exists as structurally open to the spirit of another person, it is structurally open to the Spirit of God. When we speak of spirituality as a relation with God we are speaking of the social spirituality which is constitutive of the human person, not a religious instinct, feeling, or practice. Social spirituality is what makes religion possible. Social spirituality is not only the source of authentic relation with God; it is also the first casualty of sin and in need of redemption.

Mental illness as lack of spiritual fitness

We might now speak of mental illness as a lack of spiritual fitness. In saying this, I do not mean to ignore the fact that recent discoveries in the mental health field indicate that much mental illness has a biological/

chemical origin for which pharmaceutical aid has proven helpful. At the same time, my focus is on the overall effect of mental illness in terms of the unity and integration of the self, not merely on the causes.

In addition to healing for deep intra-psychic disturbances, emotional pain, and dysfunctional social relationships, the self requires mending at the level of core social spirituality. When the spiritual core of the self is broken at the root, there is need of grace as a spiritual palliative as well as therapeutic relief. In his play *The Great God Brown* Eugene O'Neill (1982) has one of his characters say: 'We are born broken. We live by mending. The grace of God is the glue' (p.318).

The Jesuit psychotherapist, W.W. Meissner (1987) says 'Grace not only alters our theological condition, but it delves into our psychic reality... Grace is the energizing and relational principle on the spiritual level for the proper functions of the ego. Development of spiritual identity, then, is achieved through the same ego-functions that are involved in the natural psychological identity' (pp.7, 58). Facilitating a movement toward health in one sphere may release the self to grow toward health in another sphere. The 'ego' as a specific subject of psychological attention lies between the self and its lived experience in the world. When the self is addressed and responds at the level of its spiritual sphere, the 'ego' of the self is also touched and healed. Effective mediation of God's grace not only is a spiritual means for healing, it also touches the very core of the human self, enabling it and assisting it in the integrative task of becoming whole.

What the Apostle Paul calls the 'works of the flesh' as contrasted with the 'fruit of the Spirit' are symptomatic of negative and pathological social spirituality – enmities, strife, jealousy, anger, quarrels, dissensions, factions (Galatians 5:20). These are some of the diagnostic categories by which the Bible identifies sin: not first of all violations of an abstract moral law, but the breakdown of the social spirituality which is necessary for healthy marriage and family life, as well as other social relations. The therapeutic effects of spiritual fitness through the indwelling of the Holy Spirit are likewise described in terms of healthy social spirituality – love, joy, peace, patience, kindness, generosity, faithfulness, gentleness, self-control (Galatians 5:22–23).

The epigenetic nature of personal, social being

There is something of an epigenetic factor in the relationship between social, personal, and spiritual being. It was Erik Erickson (1950), along with Lyman Wynne *et al.* (1986), who took the concept of epigenesis from biology and introduced it into family therapy. In his model, the early experience of bonding and nurture was the foundation on which communication, conflict resolution and commitment developed. A breakdown in the capacity to make and keep commitments, for example, could result from inadequate tools of conflict resolution and communication, along with a lack of core bonding experiences. Therapy thus involved rebuilding from the core foundation.

The social structure of human spirituality appears to be grounded in a sense of belonging which is experienced in early bonding relationships. A sense of self-identity emerges out of this foundational social reality leading to a sense of affective wholeness, or a feeling of wellbeing with regard to one's physical, sexual, and psychical self. The movement toward wholeness and spiritual health leads to a positive sense of self-worth. Placed in an epigenetic and schematic diagram it would look like Figure 4.1.

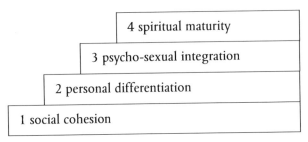

4 spiritual maturity

3 psycho-sexual integration

2 personal differentiation

1 social cohesion

1. social cohesion: a sense of belonging
2. personal differentiation: a sense of self-identity
3. psycho-sexual integration: a sense of affective wholeness
4. spiritual maturity: a sense of self-worth

Figure 4.1 An epigenetic model of human development

The epigenetic relation in Figure 4.1 means that spiritual immaturity may reflect inadequate development of psycho-sexual integration, personal differentiation, or even foundational social cohesion. Spiritual fitness, thus, begins with a sense of belonging issuing out of social cohesion.

It follows from this that spiritual fitness (mental health) must necessarily include the development of human personhood as social being. The core social paradigm of human existence includes spiritual formation as much as it does physical and personal existence.

The recovery of personal and spiritual wholeness

In the case of Ian, the presenting problem appeared to be sexual in nature, indicated by his arrest for indecent exposure. In fact, Ian himself understood it in this way. Having no explanation as to why he did such a thing, he attempted to separate himself from the act as due to something alien and uncontrollable. 'I really hate myself for having sexual desires and thoughts that I cannot control.'

Sensing that his shame and self-hatred were deeper than the result of this one incident, I asked, 'Did your parents ever catch you doing something wrong, and how did that make you feel?' Ian responded quickly, 'More often than I want to remember. One time especially, my mother walked into my room when I was masturbating, and told me that I was violating my own body and that I ought to be ashamed of myself. She said that if I kept that up I would end up just like my father, always thinking about sex. I guess that she was right. Maybe I am just a demented person.'

I have already suggested that one way of understanding Ian's behavior is to look at it from the standpoint of the pre-theoretical model. In this model, sexuality is neither physical nor mental in and of itself, but a construct of personal and social being. Look again at Figure 2.1 (p.40).

As a developmental process, sexuality emerges experientially as differentiation at the personal level, grounded in social relationships with others. The gender differentiation at the level of self-identity also becomes a powerful sexual impulse at the physical level along with mental images which become part of a stimulus response function of the brain. At this point, in the case of Ian, it appears that sexuality became split off from the social and personal aspects of self-identity with the result that a lack of integration occurred. His spiritual life became largely mental, reinforced by a highly structured religious life and a strongly held set of doctrinal beliefs. On the one hand, he was a husband and father, fulfilling those roles rather effectively as a social function. On the other hand, he was affirmed by his fellow church members as having leadership skills and a strong Christian witness. What remained invisible was the lack of integrative connection between these social and religious roles, each with a mental and physical component, and his spiritual self. Spirituality for Ian had become a calculable and manageable compartment alongside his social and physical life.

The compartmentalization of the self

As we move from the pre-theoretical model to the ecological model discussed in the previous chapter, we begin to understand how the physical, social and spiritual spheres, not being connected to each other, can result in compartmentalization within the self. Figure 4.2 shows how the model would appear without the ecological connections.

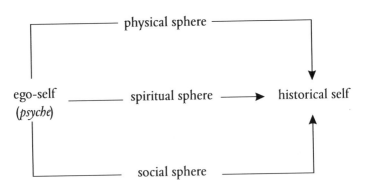

Figure 4.2 The compartmentalized self

At the historical level (real time) Ian has split his ego-self into three compartments, each developed rather effectively into roles that he could perform so as to give the appearance to others (and to himself) of being a complete person. Note that in Figure 4.2 there is no interaction between the physical, spiritual and social spheres of the self. The ecological and systematic balance has been broken and will need repair.

The recovery of spiritual wholeness

As diagnostic tools, the pre-theoretical model as well as the ecological model help us to see the lack of integration and point toward some repair work which needs to be done if Ian is to recover spiritual wholeness. The epigenetic model, Figure 4.1, helps us to see how this repair and rebuilding of a more effective life of the self can take place. The acting out of the sexual problem is not the cause of Ian's dysfunction but the result of a more basic dysfunction at the social and personal level. The focus of intervention and therapy needs to be at the foundational level of social cohesion and then personal differentiation. Clinical therapeutic intervention by a professional psychologist can be an important part of a more wholistic approach, along with pastoral care and involvement in effective personal bonding at the social level.

After referring him to a psychologist for clinical therapy, from the perspective of a practical pastoral theology I involved Ian and his wife in a process of rebuilding and rebonding at the social and personal level. In my first sessions in counseling with the couple it quickly became apparent that the role structure of their marriage – which had functioned rather effectively – had now come apart to reveal a serious lack of affective bonding and intimacy. The task was now to create new bonding relationships in which a sense of belonging and authentic self-identity could take place. Along with this and based on this, sexuality could be integrated more effectively into personal and social self-identity. Through this process, a reframing of spirituality had to take place in such a way that human and personal life of the spirit as embodied soul and ensouled body could become the seat and source of life of the Spirit in relation to God. The process of his recovery and the healing of their marital relationship took many months. Ian's wife also needed some pastoral counseling in order for her to process the forgiveness which she had too quickly proffered in order to experience the fruit of forgiveness in both herself and in her husband. At the appropriate time, I was able to involve them both in a regular support group with the church by which they could integrate the grace of God's healing power and presence with authentic social and personal community of life.

It is here that the contribution of W.W. Meissner (1987) as cited above can be appreciated. 'Grace is the energizing and relational principle on the spiritual level for the proper functions of the ego. Development of spiritual identity, then, is achieved through the same ego-functions that are involved in the natural psychological identity' (pp.7, 58). When the ego-functions of the self are split between personal identity and spiritual identity, both suffer. One cannot move toward health and wholeness at the physical/mental level while the self is fragmented at the psycho-spiritual level.

The role of the community

The role of the community of faith in spiritual formation must go beyond the inculcation of doctrinal truths and the discipline of religious practice. 'Spirituality is a Domestic Skill,' as I have written elsewhere (Anderson 1985, pp.115–128). The church as a community committed to the formation of the spiritual life of its members must first of all have a biblical theology of spirituality which takes into account the life and function of persons in their primary relationships, family, friends, and the workplace. Each of the Apostle Paul's admonitions concerning the practice of living by the Spirit focuses primarily on what I call domestic relationships rather than on how people perform in church or in the practice of religion. Spirituality is measured by how one treats other people – not lying, not using abusive language, not being contentious. Effective spiritual fitness means bearing the fruit of the Spirit – living peaceably, forgiving one another, showing mercy, and building up others in love (for example, Romans 12:9–21; Galatians 5:16–26; Ephesians 4:26–32; Colossians 3:5–13).

These instructions ought to form the curriculum of a practical theology of spiritual and personal health and wholeness. For the church's preaching and teaching ministry to be effective, access to the daily and personal lives of its members must be available without violating the integrity of these relationships. Entering into the community of faith should include the expectation that the quality of life and love which takes place with others in daily life is a matter of concern to all members of the community. The practice of friendship, for example, as John Swinton (2000b) has reminded us, is a spiritual component of the community as the body of Christ and has therapeutic as well as religious value in the promotion of health and wholeness.

At this point we are moving toward a view of human development which is grounded in what I call a life continuum as a context for spiritual as well as personal growth and maturity. In the chapter which follows I will develop this more fully.

5

The Life Continuum and the Formation of Self-Identity

Susie is a former student and my friend. Afflicted with cerebral palsy since birth, she cannot dress or feed herself. She talks with difficulty and in words which emerge as twisted and tortured as she forces them out. With a passion for life that exceeds most others less restrained by birth boundaries of their own, she completed college and a master's degree in theology, including several courses sitting in my classes. When she received her degree, I questioned her as to what she intended to do, perceiving her within the boundaries which I had set for her. 'Perhaps you will have a significant ministry to others who suffer handicaps in life,' I suggested. 'No,' she said, 'most of them haven't forgiven God for who they are, and I have.'

Forgiving God for who I am! Indeed! Whom should she hold responsible for the constricting birth boundaries which imprisoned her free and joyous spirit within a body she could not control? She expanded the horizon of her complaint, like Job of old, and laid the offense at the throne of God. When the Lord who created her did not dodge or duck, she concluded that the only freeing thing left was to forgive. Having lodged the charge against God with all of the emotional power at her disposal, she discovered that she also had the capacity to forgive him.

Susie had no sense that God had caused her birth deformity nor did she feel that he had willed this condition for some inscrutable purpose of his own. Her dealings with God were not theological but deeply existential. She sought to touch with her feelings the face of God and trace out there the profile of one who would take responsibility for her life without looking away. What she found encouraged her that, in holding God responsible, she found an ally in her predicament.

Releasing God from blame became possible when God assumed responsibility. Her life now had two sides to it. The one side of her life was restricting and confining. The other side was open and freeing. This is what she meant by forgiving God for who she was. She let God become the other side to her life. She made the outward journey and discovered a new horizon for her inner self.

In this chapter I will present the concept of a life continuum as a process through which persons discover their self-identity. From birth to death, the human person is on a trajectory of growth which involves the three ecological spheres, as developed in Chapter 3. The physical, social and spiritual spheres each require a positive environment in which to experience optimal growth and health. At the same time, each sphere contributes to and interacts with each other sphere.

Spiritual growth will then be shown to be contiguous with personal growth, with therapeutic strategies of intervention grounded in the ongoing therapeutic process of human development.

The concept of self

While practical theology requires the concept of the self in much the same way as does moral philosophy or clinical psychology, the primary concern is not so much for a phenomenological description as for an ontological designation. Let me explain. We are concerned first of all for the nature of human personhood, as has been presented in the first chapter of this book. The biblical tradition defines humanity as created in God's image and likeness, differentiated as male and female (Genesis 1:26–27). This differentiation is grounded in a social structure of personal being and relationship in which the divine image is represented as a spiritual orientation, a qualitative distinction, and gracious endowment. By ontological is meant a quality of personal *being*. A phenomenological description of human life, by contrast, tends to focus on behavior rather than being. The biblical concept of the divine image and likeness can be understood as a determination of human *being* rather than merely functional characteristics of human behavior.

Created in the image of God, who is considered to be the quintessence of personal being, humans are held to be inherently personal. Violation of this personal being unique to each individual carries with it severe consequences (see Genesis 9:6; Matthew 18:6). Some Christian theorists adopt a functional view of the self and deny that the self is an internal organ of identity, but only a 'theory which persons have about themselves' (McFadyen 1990). This concept, however, appears to undercut the biblical emphasis on the self as an essential and not merely functional attribute of personal existence.

As to the concept of 'self,' the Bible rarely uses the word in the sense of self-life. In the New Testament, the major instance is the phrase 'deny yourself' (Matthew 16:24; Mark 8:34; Luke 9:23). These three passages refer to the same incident in which Jesus reminds his disciples that, like his own devotion to the service of God, they too must be willing to turn away from the kind of self-preoccupation that leads to loss of life. Jesus teaches that to *gain* life requires investment in daily commitment to God's sovereign will. The 'old self' (Romans 6:6; sometimes called 'flesh' by Paul, Romans 7:18) is devoted to self-interest, while the 'new self' (Ephesians 4:24; Colossians 3:10, sometimes spoken of as being 'raised with Christ'; Ephesians 2:5–6) is devoted to self-fulfillment and realization of one's deepest longings and eternal joy through the indwelling Holy Spirit. In the vocabulary of the New Testament, self can mean negatively the egocentric self-life, but it can also mean positively the person's soul or spirit which is of inestimable value both to God and therefore to oneself. We are to love God with all of our heart, soul, strength, and mind, and 'our neighbor as ourselves' (Matthew 22:39).

Self-identity and the image of God

I have argued above (Chapter 2) that, while the image of God as the total self must be acknowledged as fully present from the beginning of the human person, the *content* of this image is only realized through a development process. Self-identity, then, is acquired as the particular form of the image of God resulting from the growth and development of the self in the threefold ecological spheres of physical, social, and spiritual being in the world. The divine image which constitutes humans as created by God can be understood as developmental in nature, though present as an incipient quality of life from the very beginning.

At the same time, as Martin Lang (1983) suggests, the process of coming to self-identity as created in God's image is also a matter of 'choosing' one's God as an act of love and emotion. 'The choice of "one's

God" within a story-myth is an emotional choice. It is a matter of feeling, of fidelity, of love. The bonding capacity, the capacity for love that has been learned and nourished in childhood, is brought into the selection. Relating to one's God is a matter of *loving* choice' (p.84).

The growth of the person into a self-identity which is wholistic and integrated will ordinarily take place in a context of social and spiritual interaction. This integration is part of the construct of an I–Thou experience. The mental and physical dimensions of the self are correlated through the openness of the self toward a transcending subject (self) or, in personal terms, a transcending object.

James Loder (1989) describes the process by which the self experiences a 'transforming moment' as 'therapeutic knowing.' 'In therapeutic knowing, transformational logic is transposed into a context in which the self undergoes transformation.' Loder goes on to say, 'The gift is the knowledge of oneself, including as the essential ingredient the freedom to choose for the self one has come to know.' This involves what Loder calls a 'transformation sequence.' 'That is, it must work through to congruence and correspondence to ensure the continuity of intentionality with respect to the original conflict' (pp.57–62).

The formation of self: transforming moments

My friend Susie experienced what Loder has called a transforming moment when she came to a 'therapeutic knowing' of herself as God's child even though severely limited through a physical disability. This was not a one time only experience but a process by which her self-identity became congruent with her destiny. Loder describes the process in this way.

> In sum, we live an increasingly fragile, fascinating, and creative life precisely as we take up and exert that with which we are already endowed at birth, the capacity to compose the 'world.' Being human means not only being destined to compose, but also choosing for one's destiny; the human being either risks 'world' composition or loses the sense of what it means 'to be.' (p.73)

Susie 'chose her destiny' and 'composed her world' and thus found liberation to experience creativity and self-fulfillment within the boundaries of her physical limitations. The spiritual ecology of her life became healthy and she experienced wholeness as she 'composed' her own world, as Loder puts it.

Charles Gerkin (1984) describes the process as a 'hermeneutical' one, a matter of interpreting one's world as it is experienced. The self emerges through this process, says Gerkin, as having continuity through the stages of life and by gaining the capacity to interpret (or compose) the events that happen to the self.

> To use the designation self is to emphasize the line of experienced continuity and interpretive capacity which emerges from the self's object relations... To extend D.W. Winnicott's language, it is the role of interpretation to sustain and solidify the line of continuing existence that provides the self with a sense of continuity at all levels of its functioning. The line of life becomes a line of interpretation – the hermeneutics of the self. Within a theological perspective I would place that process at the center of the life of the soul in all its relationships. (pp.98, 102)

Through the transitional stages of development from infancy to adulthood and to the end of life, the sanity and health of the person is preserved through experienced continuity of self-identity. Failure to maintain this continuity can lead to a breakdown in mental health. In severe cases, it may even require institutionalization. We judge the sanity of people by the degree to which they can identify themselves with their own history. Second, events take place along the way which require interpretation as to what possible meaning they hold for the person who experiences them. This is what Gerkin calls the 'hermeneutics of the self.' This is why he speaks of the self as a 'living human document.' The document which comprises our life is composed, to use Loder's term, as the self maintains connection with past experiences while, at the same time, integrating new ones.

Being the self in the face of disability

'I am *not* dying of AIDS; I am living with AIDS,' protested Andrew, who was being interviewed for a news feature on the effects of the disease. Statistically his distinction was not very significant. Of 20 of his acquaintances who were diagnosed with the disease one year ago, only six were still living. Why did Andrew cling stubbornly to a perspective of living with an incurable disease as opposed to dying from it? Is he permitted this illusion simply for the sake of preserving his personal dignity and emotional stability? Will his attitude affect the inevitable outcome? Will he buy more time through this 'therapeutic knowing' (Loder 1989) and gain more days, months, years?

He was unable to answer these questions. Nor can anyone else. For the questions miss the mark. He saw his life as a structure of reality over which he retained control by integrating one new, though terrible, factor – his disease – into the whole of his life. He refused to think of himself as a victim, or as a diseased person, or even a dying one, though he was not in denial of the reality of death as the final outcome. But he retained 'script rights' over the story of his life! This is what Gerkin means by an 'interpretive capacity,' and what Loder means by a 'transforming moment.'

Susie told me that she is going to write a book sharing her perspective on life with others. The opening chapter is titled 'Being Normal in an Abnormal World.' For her, those who can walk without falling, put food in their mouth without help, and talk without groaning out each word were 'abnormal.' That is, they were living outside of the world that she experienced as 'normal.' Not to be dependent upon another person and to be free to live completely independent of the care and concern of others, seemed abnormal to her. She experienced life as an ecological dynamic of physical, social, and spiritual interaction, and she had already composed the document before putting a word on paper!

Susie's physical limitations intensified the degree of social relatedness in terms of needing daily care in performing the most ordinary and simple tasks in life. Rather than this being a 'handicap' for her and others, it led to a deeper and more enriching experience of personal being both on her part and on the part of those who cared for her. In this way, the ecological dimension of her self-experience transformed what would seem to be a severe limitation into a significant spiritual experience of love and happiness. As I attended her wedding to a man who entered into this transforming experience with her not only as caretaker but also as friend, lover, and companion, I gained new insight into the capacity of the human self to create and sustain health and wholeness in sometimes difficult and demanding situations.

The social construct of the self

Disagree

I have argued that the human self as created in the image of God is essentially social in nature (Anderson 1982). It follows, then, that the self's encounter with other selves has an effect in shaping the inner life of the self that is quite unique and unparalleled by any other encounter. Theologian Wolfhart Pannenberg (1985, p.259) points to the essential social construct of the self when he says, 'In human beings, who are in a special way social beings, the self-transcendence of the affective life is largely oriented to the social environment. The positive affects, in which individuals open themselves to their world, are ecstatically inserted into inter-human relations.' John Macmurray (1935) adds a significant comment: 'The promise of the full maturity of religion in human life is put perfectly in Paul's words: "Then shall I know even as also I am known"; and it is the core of his paean in praise of love. It expresses the perfect and complete mutuality of communion, of mutual emotional awareness' (p.63).

The self in a community of love

The priority of the social relation in the differentiation of the self is a direct implication of the image of God as grounded in co-humanity rather than in individuality. The awakening of the infant to selfhood and the beginning of the development of the image of God as a possibility and personal history of fulfillment are linked to the encounter with others. This begins at the earliest point of the infant's life, and the 'face' that shines upon the infant in love reflects and mediates the love of God, a point articulated eloquently by Hans Urs von Balthasar (1967):

> No man reaches the core and ground of his own being, becoming free to himself and to all beings, unless love shines on him... God, who inclined toward his new-born creature with infinite personal love, in order to inspire him with it and to awaken the response to it in him, does in the divine supernatural order something similar to a mother. Out of the strength of her own heart she awakens love in her child in true creative activity... The essential thing is, that the child, awakened thus to love, and already endowed by another's power of love, awakens also to himself and to his true freedom, which is in fact the freedom of loving transcendence of his narrow individuality. (p.87)

This first experience of love is obviously experienced as a depth of feeling before it comes to expression as an intention. If the self should be impoverished of these feelings, its emotional life will be narrow and rigid. The 'narrow individuality' of which von Balthasar speaks describes all too well the isolation of the self which has failed to integrate feelings with intentions. The emotions remain trapped within a pattern of self-attribution so that attempts to form effective and lasting relationships, despite the best of intentions undergirded with sacred vows, continually fail. Pannenberg (1985) explains why this is so:

> The orientation of human beings to a fullness of life that transcends them and manifests itself especially in the community of their fellow human beings finds expression in the positive affects and passions, especially in feelings of sympathy but also in joy and hope. These draw individuals out of their isolation and therefore may not be simply condemned as expressions of human egocentricity. On the other hand, it is characteristic of such affects, moods, and passions as are negatively related to the environment and other people (fear, anxiety, arrogance, sadness, envy, and hate) that they isolate individuals within themselves. The positive affects and passions, on the contrary, must be understood as expressions of an 'anticipatory expectation' in which the human being is aware of the 'positive or negative termination into which the value of his being necessarily flows.' (p.265)

The role of feelings

Because love is attributed to God as the essence of divine motivation and action, it is also the core expression of the image of God in humans. Love is not only an act of volition, says the theologian Emil Brunner (1979) but also an expression of *feeling*. To the Western mind, with its European bent toward the abstract, the contrast between feeling and intellect is an assumed dichotomy in the self. Feelings, and therefore experience, are discounted as subjective and unreliable. In the biblical perspective, however, feelings are located at the core of the self in its orientation toward God and the other.

> Feeling therefore has its rightful place in man's 'experience' of his relation with God, because this 'experience' is something which man has received, and not something which he has created. To be apprehended by the love

of God, means to be smitten in the very centre of one's being, to suffer it, not as pain, but as the supreme joy, as happiness and peace; that is, the Self knows that it is 'at home' in God, and that the 'I' and the 'Self' have become one. (p.227)

Genuine feeling, Brunner adds,

> is not possible without spirit, for feelings arise out of the spiritual depths of the self, not merely as emotional reactions. A good meal does not arouse joy in the eater, but only gives pleasure to the senses. If one eats with joy it is because the spirit is turned toward another spirit, as the apostle Paul wrote: 'So whether you eat or drink, or whatever you do, do everything for the glory of God' (1 Corinthians 10:31). Through joy, pleasure is lifted to a higher plane since the self is touched at its deepest core.

The self has its own emotions, to be sure. But these emotions were conditioned from the beginning by the stimulation of feelings in the self by contact with others. With the fall into sin, the original unity of feeling with love and knowledge was severed, resulting in the psychological separation of feeling from the spirit. The severance of pleasure from relation to God means that the self is abandoned to the world of the senses. Thus Brunner goes on to say:

> In his feeling he is completely passive; he has no power over his feeling, the disharmony of his existence comes out in his feeling, against his will, while in thought and will, to some extent at least, he is able to go beyond himself. His feeling as a whole is the total balance of his existence which is drawn up and presented to him without his will... This unstilled longing for life, this negative balance of life, is therefore in the Bible everywhere the most important point of contact for the Gospel message: 'If any man thirst let him unto Me and drink' (John 7:37). (pp.233–34)

The other person provides the necessary boundary, or resistance, for the self to be differentiated in a relation of mutual trust and acceptance. When we give priority to self-reflection and self-consciousness in abstraction from relation to the other, our movements toward others will be cautious and even mistrustful. 'I need you to be myself,' says John Macmurray (1961).

If we quarrel…we can no longer be ourselves in relation to one another. We are in conflict, and each of us loses his freedom and must act under constraint. There are two ways in which this situation can be met without actually breaking the relationship – which, we are assuming, is a necessary one. There may be a reconciliation which restores the original confidence; the negative motivation may be overcome and the positive relation re-established. Or we may agree to co-operate on conditions which impose a restraint upon each of us, and which prevent the outbreak of active hostility. The negative motivation, the fear of the other, will remain, but will be suppressed. This will make possible co-operation for such ends as each of us has an interest in achieving. But we will remain isolated individuals, and the co-operation between us, though it may appear to satisfy our need of one another, will not really satisfy *us*. For what we really need is to care for one another, and we are only caring for ourselves. We have achieved society, but not community. We have become associates, but not friends. (p.150)

This is an echo of the words of Martin Buber (1979), who wrote that the concept of self emerges only through encounter with the other (p.62). Stanley Hauerwas (1981) reminds us that self-identity is not something that we can create for ourselves, by our own efforts; it is a gift. 'The necessary existence of the other for my own self is but a reminder that the self is not something we create, but is as gift. Thus we become who we are through the embodiment of the story in the communities in which we are born.' When our identity is grounded in a community, says Hauerwas, we are grasped by the story which defines us as part of that community as that which is true. 'And at least one indication of the truthfulness of a community's story is how it forces me to live in it in a manner that gives me the skill to take responsibility for my character' (pp.148–9).

The goal of self-fulfillment

Self-fulfillment is an intrinsic need and a positive good for every person. It is when self-fulfillment becomes a craving for indulging the self that the craziness and the chaos begin. As Paul warned in his letter to the Christians in Rome, when we turn away from our spiritual origin and destiny in God and become obsessed with our created human nature, we become 'foolish, faithless, heartless, ruthless' (Romans 1:31). This kind of self-indulgence leads to the dehumanization of others and the deteriorization of our own spiritual existence.

The positive direction of self-fulfillment moves toward the spirit of the other with openness, trust and a commitment to uphold the humanity and spiritual life of the other. When we find the spirit of another person matching and meeting our own spirit, then we have discovered true fulfillment. The move toward self-fulfillment, however, meets with resistance when the self encounters the will of the other self. While the social construct of human personhood is essential for there to be authentic selfhood, it is also in this social relation that the self encounters resistance.

From self-gratification to self-fulfillment

The encounter of the self with other selves is experienced as resistance to what I called the 'ego-self' in the previous chapter. This resistance is encountered early in the infant's development and experienced as a threat to self-gratification and also as a loss of power to fulfill one's own needs and desires.

This sense of being 'all-powerful' is an acquired feeling, it is not innate such as is the pleasure instinct. We are not born with a sense of power, but each of us possesses from birth a need for self-fulfillment. At the core of the pleasure instinct is a deep longing for the fulfillment of self through relation to another. This 'God-created' longing seeks fulfillment in its source; that is the love of God. Human love and relation is a reflection of that divine image which is experienced as a longing and desire for self-fulfillment. There is, in a sense, a 'moral right' to this fulfillment, so that if it is denied there is a sense of violation and even injury to the self. The earliest experience of this longing for self-fulfillment is the pleasure instinct in the child. The feeling of omnipotence for the child becomes attached to a sense of ownership of space, toys, and even persons.

The newborn infant certainly possesses an ego-self, though largely undeveloped. This ego-self is the seat of feelings (emotions) and the core of what will become self-identity. The infant first of all experiences at a subconscious level a social relation with the primary caretaker(s) through which differentiation at the personal and sexual level gradually emerges. Through this process the full range of psychical feelings and responses are developed from their original limited capacity. The core of the self as spiritual being, which from the beginning has been in place, now is opened up to response to God and to the other. The egocentrism of the self, present from the beginning, is thus developed simultaneously with the self's development of social identity. The process of development is not from egocentric to social perspectival as much as it is from immature self to mature self-identity, both as egocentric and social relating.

Healing deep wounds to the self

For the infant, gratification and fulfillment are fused and undifferentiated. When resistance is encountered to self-gratification the infantile self feels powerless and threatened. When the infant's expressed need for self-gratification is resisted by the caretaker, it is not only experienced as denial of pleasure, but also as loss of power. This feeling of powerlessness, at not being able to find immediate gratification of the pleasure instinct, causes a variety of compensatory mechanisms to kick in. The goal of these mechanisms is to manipulate the source of gratification and produce a response. A new set of behavior patterns is quickly learned and reinforced by the caregiver's adaptation to the demands. The infant is soon back in control of its environment and the core narcissistic needs are being fulfilled.

At the age of two years, my grandson Brandon had what I considered to be his fair share of toys. As I observed him playing outside with the neighbor children, there appeared to be a fair ecological balance within that general age-group. But as I watched them happily playing, it soon became apparent that happiness is a fragile experience in the toyland of childhood.

It was the yellow car in which Thomas sat that captured the imagination of Brandon. Walking right up to it, he attempted to push Thomas out and crawl in himself. The consternation on the face of Thomas was only exceeded by the bright-eyed zeal in the eyes of Brandon who, despite being outpointed in months and size, sought to take physical ownership of what had already become his by desire. The result? Two unhappy little boys. One denied access to a toy he truly needed in order to be happy; the other desperately gripping the steering wheel of a car that was now secured with fear and trembling. The fun had gone out of the toy. It was now a possession to be defended against the unprovoked terrorism of his little friend. Would he ever again be able to play happily with his little yellow car without a sense of fear that he could lose it in a moment to his closest playmate? And how about Brandon? Will his stable of toys be sufficient now that he has been denied the one thing on which his heart was set?

The fact that a few hours later both boys were happily playing together (the yellow car had been confiscated by parental discretion) reminds us of how quickly happiness can be restored when the attention span is short. And yet, one suspects that a lesson had been learned – someone else always has more toys! This is the first lesson of childhood unhappiness. Life is not fair. What your heart desires your hands cannot acquire. What is rightfully yours can be lost to another.

When violation of the self leads to moral outrage

When that which is deemed necessary for one's pleasure is denied, either by confiscation or negation, it is not experienced as delayed gratification of pleasure but as a violation of one's right of ownership. When the yellow car is confiscated, both Brandon and Thomas are offended, each in his own way. No compromise can be accepted and no promise of future pleasure will suffice. For the immediate sensation is outrage over a violation of what each feels is rightfully his, not only loss of pleasure.

In some cases, children can be coaxed out of their temper tantrum by an immediate offer of an even greater gratification – a double-dip ice-cream cone, for instance! This, however, only compounds the problem. The use of pleasure to alleviate a sense of moral outrage is a 'quick fix' of happiness, leaving the underlying unhappiness unhealed and untouched. There is a deeper longing which remains unfulfilled.

When the self acquires the feeling of being in control and having ownership of what is needed for self-gratification, the moral instinct shifts from pleasure to power of ownership. When the desire for pleasure is frustrated it is perceived as a threat to the moral right to possess that which is needed for one's gratification. The instinct to recover one's control over the situation can lead to abuse of the rights and person of others. The culmination of this process in acts of violence brings moral condemnation on the abuser.

'When I was a child,' the Apostle Paul wrote, 'I thought like a child and reasoned like a child' (1 Corinthians 13:11). From our own experience we can gain some insight into what he meant. In a 'childish' way of thinking and reasoning, a 'bird in the hand is worth two in a bush,' as proverbial wisdom puts it. Promise a two-year-old boy a new toy as compensation for giving up his immediate possession of the TV remote control, and you have added nothing to balance the scales of justice in his mind. The child's sense of values is weighted heavily in favor of that which provides immediate gratification.

Dealing with infantile narcissism

This is rooted in what I have called 'infantile narcissism,' the self-love of the child. The intrinsic longing for self-fulfillment comes to expression first as a feeling of gratification when immediate needs are met. The capacity for delayed gratification of these needs for the sake of a more lasting and cherished form of self-fulfillment is one mark of growth and maturity. 'When I became an adult,' Paul testified, 'I put an end to childish ways.' As a result, he concluded, 'faith, hope, and love abide, these three; and the greatest of these is love' (1 Corinthians 13:11, 13).

The psychotherapist, William Meissner (1987) suggests that there is a 'childhood narcissism' which is essential to personal well-being in the adult. Experienced losses to this narcissistic core play a critical role in psychic development.

> The sense of loss and diminished self-esteem attack the fundamental narcissism at the root of our emotional lives. This narcissism is essential to our psychological well-being and any threat to it must be resisted. And so loss sets in motion restorative efforts by which the ego strives to recover the loss and reconstitute the sense of self-esteem. Self-esteem is a fragile but indispensable vessel, whose preservation requires care and constant effort in the face of the onslaughts of deprivation and loss. (p.140)

This 'fundamental narcissism' is what I have called 'infantile narcissism' because it appears in its most delightful and healthy form in infants. We do not scold infants for this innate pleasure instinct but encourage and reward it. It is only when the infant grows into a child and then into an adult that this instinct for self-pleasure becomes a source of irritation and disapproval by others. I use the phrase 'infantile narcissism' intentionally in order to suggest that narcissism itself is not a negative attribute of the self and, second, to trace out the developmental process by which this fundamental narcissism can be empowered to become the positive basis for self-esteem.

Narcissism is not sinful

A serious mistake can be made in a theology of the self by equating the sinful self with the narcissistic self. Theologians who claim that all children are born with an inherited sin nature, called original sin, are often tempted to view the self as totally without value, with every instinct of the self corrupted and disposed toward wrongdoing. The redemption of the self, then, entails a replacement of this sinful self with a new self, grounded in the grace of God.

I too hold that every person is born with a disposition toward sin, but that this disposition is not located in the instinct for self-fulfillment and pleasure but in the instinct to use power over others and one's own life to gain that fulfillment. The image of God with which each person is endowed is the source for positive self-worth and self-fulfillment. This is the infant's capacity to love itself, which I have called infantile narcissism.

Original sin, however one defines it theologically, is the condition of every human person by which the infantile narcissism is fused with an instinct to control and gain power so as to provide one's own self with pleasure and fulfillment. Original sin may be posited as a sense of omnipotence which is fused with the narcissistic instinct giving the infant a sense of absolute power over others who cater to the infant's every need. Self-fulfillment is quite different from self-gratification. Furthermore, as Meissner has indicated, this fundamental narcissism must be transformed (Loder 1989) into a mature form of pleasure attained through self-fulfillment.

The image of God and original sin must be differentiated clearly so that the core of the self is not *essentially* destroyed by sin. This is important for psychological reasons as well as theological ones. The psychology of self-identity requires a thread of continuity through even the most severe forms of mental illness and emotional disorder. The theology of self-identity likewise requires continuity through the radical experience of new birth and spiritual renewal. Theology has tended to be more concerned with the eradication of sin and the implanting of a 'new nature' than preserving the self. Psychology has tended to be more concerned with restoring the self than with providing a 'new nature' through spiritual conversion. Both theologians and psychologists need to consider the inherent value and potential of the human self as created in God's image. The effect of God's grace and spiritual renewal is to free the self from compulsive and irrational need to control and satisfy the need for self-gratification through inappropriate use of manipulation and power.

The grace of empowerment

With the intervention of the grace of God the infantile narcissism is freed from the need to control and is empowered by love to experience self-worth. The intervention of divine grace may be seen as providing empowerment for the self to retain the infantile narcissism in the form of self-worth, or self-esteem, with delayed gratification the evidence of this 'fruit of the Spirit.' Tolerance for delayed gratification is the mark of growth and maturity resulting in qualities of life which lead to Shalom – the Hebrew word for peace, health, wholeness, and reconciliation.

The integration of psychological concerns for health and wholeness coincide with theological concerns for a spirituality which is also the recovery of the true humanity of the self. In the same way, theological concerns for the effects of sin arising out of the self merge with psychological concerns for dysfunctional and disruptive behavior at the personal and social level.

Empowerment of the self must come from a source outside the self. This is not only a theological truth but also a psychological reality, as the 'relational' psychologists have told us. The emergence of psychologies based on interpersonal constructs of the self point toward a dynamic of empowerment as a source of self-esteem. When, instead of resistance to the self, which produces negative self-esteem, the self experiences positive reinforcement, we find the pathway to self-recovery opened up.

Sooner or later, all children moving into adulthood will be confronted by experiences which require the surrender of right of ownership for the sake of self-fulfillment. At these times, there needs to be a shift which will feel unfamiliar and unnatural to the self. It is a leap of growth when the self learns to experience the moral worth and the fulfillment received through empowering the life of another.

In making this movement, the self moves away from the primitive moral instinct which has become fused with ownership to an ethic of love. We long for love which is not an innate instinct of the self but which is the highest possibility of the self. Love means acquiring the capacity to experience ultimate meaning and fulfillment of the self in the life of another. There is an innate moral right to this fulfillment, and this is the seed from which love can grow.

The empowerment of love is one form of the grace of God directed toward the self through human parents, the ministry of Christ in Word and Spirit, and the effective intervention of Christian therapists. The longing for self-fulfillment is not the root of sin. Rather, sin emerges through the inherited sense of ownership and autonomy with regard to the Word and law of God. Although a strong sense of omnipotence develops when the pleasure instinct is gratified without setting the boundaries of love, the key to fulfillment is not to annihilate the self but to rediscover the self as an object of God's love. This leads to self-worth and moral worth, with self-fulfillment gained through the intentions and actions of love.

The therapeutic potential of being human

The continuum of life as pilgrimage is a therapeutic continuum for all persons when considered from this perspective. This therapeutic continuum stretches from the most informal caregiving which takes place through domestic, community and friendship encounters to the more specialized forms of pastoral care and finally includes medical assistance and psychotherapy in a clinical setting. On this continuum, all forms of caregiving and healing are forms of intervention for the purpose of restoring persons to the on-going process of growing toward wholeness. The resources may be more narrowly defined and focussed, but the process of healing is the same. All persons get well for the same reason, regardless of the therapeutic method used. Getting well, in this case, means recovering the therapeutic process of life itself. The only source of healing is in the person being healed, though the process may depend upon skilled intervention with appropriate therapeutic methods.

The astonishing and astounding fact is this. Humanity is by its very nature therapeutic. Healing is grounded in humanity, not in the removal of pathology. To put it another way, being human requires openness of being to the other and allowance of the other to touch the core of one's own being. Adam can express it in amazingly concrete terms as 'bone of my bones and flesh of my flesh' (Genesis 2:3). This 'helping and healing' encounter integrates the self with one's own 'bones and flesh,' as well as with the other, as necessary to one's own selfhood. All subsequent therapy, whether physical, psychical, social, or spiritual, is grounded in this core therapy of being human.

6

Self-Care

A Guide to Spiritual Fitness

'Take care,' my friend said, as he turned and walked away after our lunch meeting, without waiting for a response. I reflected for a few minutes on what has become a casual ritual of parting. If I had asked him how he thought I should do this, I would probably have embarrassed him by demanding more than he intended to say. On the other hand, I would probably have been uncomfortable if he had said more than I wanted to hear!

'You need to take better care of your health,' says the medical doctor, as she writes a prescription for reducing elevated blood pressure. 'You need to take more care about what you eat,' warns the nutritionist as he submits a list of 'good and bad' foods. 'You need to take care to lower your level of stress,' advises the psychologist, as she outlines a program of relaxation techniques. 'You need to take better care of your body,' urges the physical fitness trainer, as he develops a personal plan for increasing muscle tone and decreasing body fat.

Building on the theoretical models developed in the preceding chapters, I will now apply the concepts of human wholeness to the life and ministry of professional caregivers. In this chapter I will discuss the need for those who care for others to take care of themselves, especially those who are on the front line of meeting human needs.

A plan for spiritual fitness

Human need is an insatiable and unforgiving slave master, as many who devote their lives to a ministry of caregiving have found. Seeking help from professional caregivers can potentially create a burden too great for any one person to bear. As a result, those who begin with a sense of spiritual motivation and empowerment can end up in spiritual bankruptcy, emotional crisis, social isolation, and physical distress.

Let me give a personal example of what I call spiritual fitness.

'A clergyman walks in. He's a big man, 240 pounds. He strikes the desk with his fist and says, "Look, there's nothing more boring than walking around the block. If I have to eat differently than the rest of the family, well forget it, I'm not going to! Besides, if God takes me then he takes me. Then I'll be traveling without any baggage."'

Dr Taylor, a physician concerned about clergy morale, paused, as if peering once more into the mental picture he had created for some clue, and then continued. 'Professor Anderson, here is someone who believes that if he gives himself to the work of God, God will look after him. Even if he burns himself out for God, his future is secure. What is this person really saying?'

Now it was my turn to pause. I was being asked to respond as a theologian, but I experienced an instantaneous flashback through eleven years of pastoral ministry. Quite without thinking, I replied, 'The man is experiencing a kind of "quiet despair" that can subtly creep into one's ministry, and he may even be experiencing an unconscious "death wish."'

Dr Taylor was intrigued, and I must admit that I was not a little surprised at the intensity with which I had responded. Was I diagnosing the blustering, overweight clergyman, or delving into my own psyche? I suspect that it was the latter. I remember a series of sermons I had preached from Job, and the strange sense of identity I had with him when he cried out: 'Let me have silence, and I will speak, and let come on me what may. I will take my flesh in my teeth, and put my life in my hand. See, he will kill me; I have no hope; but I will defend my ways to his face. This will be my salvation, that the godless shall not come before him' (Job 13:13–16).

Let's face it, this is frankly suicidal!

I see Job as feeling caught in an inescapable bind. He is convinced that his life is given over to God, and yet God has become his adversary. There is only one way out: risk himself to the very edge of destruction, then God himself will be his vindication and his salvation.

The Job syndrome

This is the Job syndrome: 'My ministry is slowly killing me, so I will "take my flesh in my teeth" and kill myself through my ministry. Then we shall see what God will say!' Many a minister has preached his own eulogy as a healing balm to his ulcerous soul.

Coupled with the despair over never being able to satisfy these demands upon the minister is the personal sense of inadequacy for this task, not least of which is the growing sense of spiritual inadequacy. The One who called has now disappeared into the calling itself. Left to himself or herself, the minister can only seek to atone for the sins of spiritual failure by throwing himself or herself even more into the work of the ministry.

It becomes a vicious circle. The demands of the ministry produce a sense of inadequacy. Inadequacy carries the overtone of spiritual weakness. One turns to God in desperation, seeking some relief, escape at least, if not renewal. Failing here, too, there is nothing to do but throw oneself more deeply into the work of the ministry. And the cycle repeats itself again.

Periodically, someone will intervene with a common-sense question: 'You need to take better care of yourself. Shouldn't you be concerned about your physical health?' or 'You need a day off once in a while, what do you do to relax?'

Caught in the undertow of this 'divine madness' which has seized one in the name of ministry, how does one explain that the risk of a physical, or even emotional, breakdown is almost incidental compared to the high stakes for which one is playing in the escalating demands of ministry? Can we now understand what the pastor is saying when he or she says that God will 'look after me'? Of course those who are caregivers know when they are neglecting their own physical and emotional well-being, just as they know when they are precariously close to nervous exhaustion or dangerously close to the point of 'throwing in the towel' – an expression that has its origin in the exhaustion of the boxing ring! It seems especially appropriate in this context! This is why being told, or even warned, to take care is not an effective deterrent to becoming a casualty. In a sense, this well-meaning appeal to common sense actually can compound the problem and accelerate the vicious circle.

The burn-out phenomenon

'The ministry is killing me,' such a pastor secretly knows, 'but the only way to escape with honor is to go down in flames.' The so-called 'burn-out' phenomenon among professional caregivers is not so much due to over-investment in one's work as to a lack of self-care. It is a lack of spiritual fitness; it results from a disconnect between the inner life of the self and the social and physical boundaries and limits within which one seeks to meet the demands placed on the self.

Spiritual fitness is the result of the practice of a spiritual ecology of wholistic self-care expressed in a ministry of caring for others. Spiritual fitness, like physical fitness, activates inner resources for healing, releases untapped energy, and produces a sense of personal well-being that contributes to effective relation with others, including God.

A practical theology of self-care

In developing a model of spiritual fitness, I will examine the lack of health and wholeness within the inner life of the self, and then discuss 'self-spirituality' as a promotion of the so-called New Age movement. A practical theology of caregiving in relation to one's own needs as social, physical and spiritual persons will then be presented as a basis for the achievement of spiritual fitness. This model is based on what I have discussed in previous chapters as a model for a wholistic and integrative view of the self, for the intrinsic social structure of human spirituality, and for the ecological structure of social spirituality.

The loss of soul in contemporary life

Thomas Moore's (1992) best-selling book, *Care of the Soul*, spoke to a growing concern for a spirituality of the inner life. Moore says, 'When soul is neglected, it doesn't just go away; it appears symptomatically in obsessions, addictions, violence, and loss of meaning...the root problem is that we have lost our wisdom about the soul, even our interest in it' (1992, p.xi). The literature of the 'therapy of the soul' is growing rapidly (for example, see Collins 1995; Crosby 1997; Demarest 1999; Hansen 1997; Miller 1997; Peck 1997; Webster 1999; Zukav 1989).

Lamenting the loss of a concept of a human soul among secular psychiatrists, M. Scott Peck (1997) writes, 'why is it that the word "soul" is not in the professional lexicon of psychiatrists, other mental health workers, students of the mind, and physicians in general?' His conclusion is that because 'God talk' is inherent in the concept of the soul, and 'God talk' is virtually off-limits in the secular mental profession, the soul has been ignored (p.129).

What Moore and Peck refer to as 'soul' is what I understand as the loss of an essential connectedness of persons to their own inner core of selfhood, to other persons as 'soul mates,' and to God as the source of our personal and spiritual existence. While Peck speaks of the loss of the concept and language concerning the soul, Moore refers more to an existential vacuum at the core of the self, a lack of personal vitality and value. I think of the soul not as a substance contained within the body but as the inner core of the whole person, including the body. By 'soul' I mean the personal and spiritual dimension of the self. Thus, the phrase 'body and soul' is not intended to suggest that the soul is something which is merely 'in' the body, or separate from the body, but the whole person with both an interior and an exterior life in the world (Anderson 1998). 'If the focus of the twentieth century has been on outer space, the focus of the twenty-first century may well be on inner space,' wrote the pollster George Gallop (1997, p.9).

In his book *The Denial of Death*, Ernest Becker (1975) offers insightful analysis of the neurotic and obsessive tendencies of our contemporary culture. Becker reminds us that we once lived most of our life within smaller, more cohesive communities. These communities, such as the rural village in middle America where I was raised, provided 'ready-made' rituals by which each person in the community could find a meaningful connection to others when taken by tragedy, grief, suffering, as well as in the celebrations of the mystery of birth and life. In being separated from these communities through our modern, urban, isolated, and anonymous life-style, we are forced to contrive and invent rituals to satisfy deeper anxieties personally and privately. In Becker's analysis, this accounts for neurotic obsession with private ritualistic patterns which seek to relieve anxiety and mask our dread of the unknown and unpredictable.

While Moore points to the effects of loss of soul in the symptoms of obsessions and addictions, Becker uncovers the deeper source of this loss of soul in being disconnected from the ethos and social structures that provide the rituals and mythical elements that nourish and sustain the inner life of the self. When our inner life shrinks in the face of the demands of life and the certainty of our mortality, Becker says that we seek heroic figures upon which we can project our own identity, someone larger than life, someone who bears the appearance of being immortal, even though one who also experiences suffering and tragedy. In response to the emptiness at the core of the self, some have turned to a form of self-spirituality in order to fill this vacuum.

The New Age of self-spirituality

The so-called New Age movement is less a clearly defined entity than a moving and pulsating amoebae. John Drane (1991) suggests that it may have antecedents going back as much as five hundred years but emerging more visibly and with greater vitality in our post-enlightenment, and postmodern, era. 'Anything offering the possibility of a change in human outlook is being seized upon with great enthusiasm. Elements from Eastern mysticism combine with modern psychoanalysis, meditation techniques and holistic health to produce a complex maze of pathways to personal fulfillment and wholeness' (p.45). Russell Chandler (1993) suggests that New Age is a modern revival of ancient religious traditions, drawing upon first-century Gnosticism, Eastern mysticism, modern philosophy and psychology, science and science fiction, and the counter-culture of the 1950s and 1960s (p.43).

More than anything else, the theme of spirituality pervades the movement, ranging from esoteric philosophical mysticism to sensual ecological pantheism. New Age spirituality is a parallel universe with little resemblance to more traditional forms of spirituality. If it has antecedents in certain fringe elements of traditional Christianity, such as first-century Gnosticism, it has no ancestors in the biblical story. The New Age movement has no territorial markers and no ruling authorities. Its extension is global, if not celestial. Its gospel is one of health, healing, spiritual development, and higher consciousness.

New Age spirituality is grounded in the self, often in the form of a mystical philosophy of mind and sometimes in the psychological depths of the soul. In either case, the boundary between the divine and the human becomes blurred or disappears altogether. The Judeo-Christian tradition, while viewing the human soul as bearing a divine imprint, makes a clear distinction between that which is human and that which is divine. In contrasting the New Age view with the more traditional view of humans as spiritual beings, we can note many similarities but also significant differences.

The concept of the self has experienced a new birth in the womb of New Age thought along with a concern for an inner life of spirituality. Recent studies of contemporary spirituality seem to agree that its distinctive element is some version of 'self-spirituality' (Chandler 1993; Heelas 1996; Melton et al. 1990). The self is viewed as sacred, and by making contact with the intrinsic spirituality of the self one becomes open to a spiritual world by which spiritual truth and spiritual teachers can 'channel' wisdom to the soul. Wouter Hanegraaff (1996) asserts that New Age religion, if one can even call it that, can only be seen in the mirror of Western, secular thought. It is the esoteric aspect of the New Age movement that differentiates it from the more empirical, rationalist, and reductionist views of reality in a secular view of life and the human condition.

Not only has the malaise of our contemporary society been diagnosed as loss of soul (Thomas Moore 1992); one New Age author locates the source of spiritual power for the healing of our addictions in the divine potential of the human soul. Gary Zukav (1989) says, 'You have always been because what it is that you are is God, or Divine Intelligence, but God takes on individual forms, droplets, reducing its power to small particles of individual consciousness... As that little form grows in power, in selfhood, in its own consciousness of self, it becomes larger and more Godlike. Then it becomes God' (p.186). Zukav goes on to suggest that the soul constitutes an inner core of personal being as over and against the personality and physical existence itself. The soul of every person is a smaller piece of Divine Intelligence in the process of becoming itself God. Each soul (person) is a 'reduction of an immortal Life system into the framework of time and the span of a few years' (pp.35–36).

Matthew Fox (1983), a contemporary Christian theologian and popular author identified with the New Age movement, advocates a form of 'creation spirituality.' He suggests that the persistent teaching of the 'fall/redemption' motif in traditional theology fails to satisfy the contemporary spiritual seeker. 'A devastating psychological corollary of the fall/redemption tradition is that religion with original sin as its starting point and religion built exclusively around sin and redemption does not teach trust... What if, however, religion was not meant to be built on psychologies of fear but on their opposite – on psychologies of trust and ever-growing expansion of the human person?' (p.82).

Trauma spirituality

Psychologist Robert Grant (1999) has studied the effects of trauma on victims of workplace accidents, violence, rape, and war. In his research he found that a traumatic experience can break a person, destroying trust in God and the world. Or it can provide a spiritual opening – a crack that opens the way to a deeper sense of life's meaning. Human beings, he says, have a tremendous resilience under such conditions and discover spiritual depths that lead to greater faith and hope than they have ever known. Not all have this experience, he admits, but it is more common than we realize.

From his studies, Grant concludes that there are many people who experience what he calls 'trauma spirituality.' When the fundamental beliefs and concepts upon which people have built their lives crumble and fall apart, some people allow walk through the 'metaphysical minefields' brought on by traumatic experience and emerge with an altered consciousness and new access to their spiritual core.

Spirituality in the biblical tradition

In many ways, both New Age and biblical spirituality are more alike than different when viewed from the perspective of what spirituality means when experienced and practiced. The New Age version of the self is potentially, if not actually, immortal, divine, and capable of transcending its mortal state as an earthbound creature. The biblical tradition speaks of human life as originating with a divine inbreathing which resulted in a 'living soul' (Genesis 2:7). Human being, as distinguished from all other forms of life, is said to bear the very 'image and likeness of God' (Genesis 1:26–27). The gift of life implies, at least, the gift of immortality in the biblical tradition. New Age spirituality offers freedom from the tyranny of physical needs, stress, and even disease. Through meditation, relaxation, and communion with the divine essence, persons experience healing, harmony, and hope. This is somewhat similar to what God's people are promised in the Scriptures.

For example, the wisdom literature of the Old Testament describes the state of the righteous as one of peace, prosperity, freedom from anxiety, and perfect security in the face of adversity. The 'righteous,' as contrasted with the 'wicked,' are like 'trees planted by streams of water, which yield their fruit in its season, and their leaves do not wither. In all that they do, they prosper' (Psalm 1:3). Jesus promised joy, peace, and freedom from the 'cares of this world,' to those who 'abide in him' like the branches abide in the vine (John 15:1–11). The Apostle Paul calls those who have become followers of Jesus as the Messiah 'saints' (literally 'holy ones'), and the 'living temple of God' (1 Corinthians 1:2; 2 Corinthians 6:16).

In many ways, because the focus of New Age spirituality is upon the inner transformation of the self with immediate and short-term effects of a subjective, or even physical, nature, it offers a compelling alternative to the more traditional Christian spiritual disciplines. One can receive the benefits of New Age spirituality with no membership fees, no investment in organizational duties and responsibilities, and no institutional maintenance assessments! For every dollar invested one receives at least a book to hold in one's hand and access to the practical wisdom of celebrated and acclaimed spiritual teachers. Organized religion, on the other hand, needs contributing members, not merely devoted followers.

In what way then does a more traditional, biblical approach still offer a distinctive alternative and a fulfilling life-style for the spiritual seeker? It is only when one looks for spiritual wholeness rather than merely a form of self-spirituality that one can answer that question. A spiritual cure for self-emptiness which offers health, prosperity and inner peace may yield an immediate blessing but result in an ultimate barrenness. Therapists tell me that many who experience emotional distress and mental disturbance seek immediate relief from pain rather than being willing to pursue a deeper healing which might require more pain. Ernest Becker (1975) has reminded us that 'denial of our mortality' offers short-term relief from anxiety but at the cost of authentic existence as persons who must ultimately face their own death. A form of spirituality which masks the reality of our human finitude and limitation by assuming the 'character armor' of immortality is an 'illusion that lies' (p.204). It is spiritual folly, not spiritual wisdom.

The divine image, as the biblical tradition reminds us, is not only what distinguishes us from all that is nonhuman, it is what makes us truly human as distinguished from God. Spiritual fitness is the wisdom of life lived out of the self as bearing the imprint of the divine, without being divine.

In reading the current literature on the spiritual care of the inner self, three themes keep emerging as evidence of the need for self-care. In our contemporary culture, the inner self is often described as *undernourished, overburdened,* and *disconnected.* To the extent that this is true, we may be one of the most religious societies in all the world, but also the most spiritually unfit. In what follows I want to examine each of these three areas of the life of the self and provide some guidelines for spiritual fitness.

Nourishing the inner life of the self

The overweight clergyman described by the medical doctor suffered from more than a lack of physical conditioning and proper diet. He was undernourished at the core of his inner self. When we are undernourished in this way, it may be because a great deal of popular religion is of the 'fast food' variety, highly seasoned, easily accessible and in disposable containers, requiring no preparation and little interruption of our fast-paced daily life. Purveyors of fast food have learned that people tend to prefer what is tasty rather than what is nourishing. Both the religious world and the secular world have now caught on. Everyday life is filled to excess while the inner life of the self is starving. Part of spiritual fitness is the re-education of our taste so that an appetite can be developed for that which is nourishing for the soul.

In his book *The Secret Life of the Soul* Keith Miller (1997) describes the collapse of his own frantic but highly successful life and career as an author, public speaker, and guru to evangelical groupies seeking the *Taste of New Wine* (1996). He chronicles his ascent to the heights of success and popularity followed by the downward spiral and crash resulting from the 'disconnect' between the inner life of his soul and the outer construct of the self. By his own admission, Miller was starving his soul while feeding his ego. 'In time the fruitless redoubling of our efforts to succeed seem hollow, frenetic, and ineffective. When what we are doing is not connected with who we are in our souls, redoubling our efforts can become the beginning of a subtle sort of spiritual suicide' (Miller 1997, p.105).

Signs of an undernourished soul

The signs of an undernourished soul can take many forms. Bruce Demarest (1999, p.51) suggests that the undernourished soul can suffer intellectually when asked to thrive only on thoughts rather than feelings. Or, the soul can suffer emotional deadness due to lack of strong affect such as compassion, grief, joy, or even anger. The undernourished soul can suffer relationally when the outer life becomes driven more by task and function than communion with others.

Lack of nourishment for the soul is a comparison Jesus was making when he asked: 'Is there anyone among you who, if your child asks for bread, will give a stone?' (Matthew 7:9). We all know the difference between bread and stones when it comes to physical food. Soul hunger and soul food, however, are not so easily recognized. When our inner self becomes emaciated it may not be due to lack of quantity, but of quality. People are known to have died of malnutrition while consuming large amounts of food with little or no nutritional content. Some nourishment for the inner self, however, may not depend so much on the kind of food but how it is offered and received. The undernourished self may lack a connection as much as calories.

Sitting in a chair on the walkway outside the local 'Donut Hut,' drinking my coffee on a morning break from writing, I observed the sparrows darting around picking up crumbs. They became quite bold as each rushed to pick up crumbs from around my feet. It was not just that I was a messy eater, but dropping a few crumbs intentionally provided diversion and entertainment. Each sparrow fiercely fought to get to the crumbs – no sharing among their peers! Then, as I watched, one smaller sparrow made no attempt to pick a crumb but simply fluttered its wings ever so slightly. A nearby sparrow hopped over and offered the bit of food from its own mouth directly to the mouth of the smaller sparrow. I assumed that this was the baby sparrow continuing to look to its mother for food. The size of the two sparrows appeared insignificant, as the smaller one looked quite capable of picking up crumbs for itself. The little flutter of its wings, however, was the signal which brought the mother hopping over for the feeding.

As I watched, I wondered at what point the smaller sparrow would have to pick its own crumbs and compete with the others, rather than being fed mouth-to-mouth. My guess is that the time was rapidly approaching and probably long past when this should happen. The smaller sparrow had a good thing going! As long as it made no attempt to pick its own crumbs and made the familiar gesture with the fluttering wings, it received its nourishment. Surely the smaller sparrow was reaching out for care more than for crumbs.

Nourishing care for caregivers

Too often, I fear, we live on crumbs when we should be seeking care. Each of us can find crumbs, but do crumbs truly nourish the inner self? 'One does not live by bread alone,' Jesus said, 'but by every word that comes from the mouth of God' (Matthew 4:4). The self is like a child within us, thriving on the nourishment of loving care rather than striving in competition.

As caregivers, many of us lack the kind of nourishing love which we seek to give to others. It is one thing to meditate on the Scriptures which remind us of the love that God has for us. We need more than that. We need and must cultivate relationships in which we are the recipients of the kind of love which we provide others. It is not a sign of weakness to need the love of others expressed in tangible, personal ways. Once again, the words of John Mcmurray (1961) are relevant here as a source of nourishment for the inner self: 'I need you to be myself. This need is for a fully positive personal relation in which, because we trust one another, we can think and feel and act together. Only in such a relation can we really be ourselves' (p.150).

Unburdening the inner life of the self

I have suggested that in our contemporary culture the self may often be undernourished; it can also be overburdened. Even the strongest can bend beneath burdens that are unnecessary. Spiritual fitness is not determined by how heavy a burden may be borne in life, but how well we bear the burdens that are necessary and how easily we let go of the ones that are not. The invitation of Jesus was not a promise to free us from all burdens, but to 'fit' our burden to our selves. 'Come to me, all you that are weary and are carrying heavy burdens, and I will give you rest. Take my yoke upon you, and learn from me; for I am gentle and humble in heart, and you will find rest for your souls. For my yoke is easy, and my burden is light' (Matthew 11:28–30).

Bearing the right burden

A self without a burden is immature and irresponsible. There are burdens that only we can bear, and there are burdens that can only be borne in being yoked to another. The Apostle Paul had this in mind when he wrote: 'Bear one another's burdens, and in this way you will fulfill the law of Christ. For if those who are nothing think they are something, they deceive themselves. All must test their own work; then that work, rather than their neighbor's work, will become a cause for pride. For all must carry their own loads' (Galatians 6:2–5). When we 'bear one another's burden,' we acknowledge to ourselves and to others that there are burdens that simply cannot be borne alone. At the same time, 'all must carry their own load,' for there are burdens that no one else can bear for us.

Dietrich Bonhoeffer (1985) reminded his students who were preparing to be spiritual caregivers, 'If *everything* is made subject to spiritual care, we may wind up with a lack of self-understanding. The goal of spiritual care is rather to lead people along on their own struggle to the point where they can break through it on their own. Excessive dependence on spiritual care can result in lack of resistance and inner laxity. One's own experience thus never matures, and we abandon the attempts too soon' (pp.66–67).

Letting God bear the burden of life

When we end up overburdened in life, we fall into the fallacy of thinking that we can control our lives. If we could just take on one more task, do one more thing for others, work harder on getting our own life in shape, then we could prevent the looming chaos from overtaking us and make everything come out just right. The fallacy is exposed by Jesus' rhetorical question, 'Can any of you by worrying add a single hour to your span of life? If then you are not able to do so small a thing as that, why do you worry about the rest?' (Luke 12:25, 26).

Even the lightest burden will break us if borne for the wrong reason. The burden that only we can bear has nothing to do with controlling our life and making everything work out. The burden that each of has is to 'flutter' our own wings, like the little sparrow who receives nourishment because it asks for it.

When we feel overburdened, we need to ask ourselves why we are carrying the burden of life at all, not which burdens are the right ones. The burdens which we carry by the power of faith and hope are the burdens of the sower who has no control over the harvest. Spiritual fitness is not the capability to carry heavy burdens, but the gift of faith and the vision of hope by which every burden becomes a seed sown into the soil which we cultivate and water, but for which God alone can bring the harvest.

Those of us who are caregivers, and all of us are in one way or another, need to discover which of the burdens we are carrying are ones that cannot be carried alone. There are burdens that only we can carry for ourselves. But the strength and capacity to carry these burdens results from proper nourishment as well as mutual care. Dietrich Bonhoeffer (1985) urged his students to make sure that they themselves had relationships in which they were under the care of others. 'Everyone who cares for the soul needs a person to care for his or her soul. Only one who has been under spiritual care is able to exercise spiritual care... We need someone to intercede for us daily. Those who live without spiritual care move easily toward magic and domination over others' (p.66).

The overweight clergyman suffered from personal and spiritual isolation. He not only carried too many of his own burdens, he was also carrying burdens that only others could carry for him. As a result, his inner life became disconnected from his outer life, including his ministry of caring for others. He lacked a proper spiritual ecology and was out of balance, teetering on the brink of falling into the fissures of his own sense of failure. When we become powerless to save ourselves, we tend to abuse the power we have over others.

Reconnecting the inner life of the self

When the soul is disconnected from its own source of life in the world, it will be not only undernourished and overburdened but also rendered powerless. When Keith Miller (1997) describes the recovery of his own 'loss of soul,' he distinguishes between the inner life of the self and the 'constructed personality,' which tends to be formed early in life. The constructed personality has a twofold purpose: 'The first is to quiet the shaming voices... The second purpose of the constructed personality is to represent to the world inflated constructed characteristics in order to succeed "out there."' He goes on to say, 'As long as we think our constructed personality is capable of saving us, we have unwittingly made our constructed selves God.' The disconnect between the soul and the constructed personality is like relegating the soul to prison, while developing another invisible side of our constructed personality 'that is calculating and controlling, and about which we are often in denial' (pp.67, 119, 99–100).

Unmasking the pseudo-self

Miller (1997) views the core of personal selfhood as the source of authentic feeling, emotion, and love. The constructed personality for Miller is a kind of 'pseudo-self,' constructed so as to protect the inner self from shame, vulnerability, and powerlessness. The constructed personality can function quite effectively in both the secular and religious world as long as it maintains the façade of success through posturing and performance. In Miller's case, he simply broke down under the burden of living out of his constructed personality and began to release his inner self 'from prison,' so to speak.

In his own words:

> I know that in a way, I have just begun the spiritual adventure in my soul. I know that I'll always have inner battles and that there will continue to be new revelations, crises, and surrenders in the ongoing life of my soul. But now I have new tools, weapons to face and change the self-defeating adversaries of fear, inadequacy, denial, and self-doubt. (pp.207–8)

Rather than making constant repairs to his constructed personality, Miller has begun to care for his inner self. While he at one time was highly successful as one who wrote and lectured about spirituality, he has now found the way toward the spiritual fitness that he lacked. He excelled at picking up crumbs, winning every competition, rising to the top. In the process he became overburdened and undernourished. The disconnect between his inner self and his public life produced emotional pain and spiritual bankruptcy. He has now begun to nourish and care for his real self rather than merely feed his ego.

The spirituality of the New Age movement tends to disconnect the 'higher self' from the 'lower self' in an attempt to escape the pull of gravity which anchors the self to an earthbound and temporal existence. Wholeness and health come with spiritual fitness which brings wisdom and grace into life.

The strength of spiritual fitness

Spiritual fitness continues to connect with the reality of life even when it sometimes brings pain and causes stress. Spiritual fitness empowers us to bear the heavy burdens of life rather than to choose those which feel weightless but may also be contentless. Spiritual fitness is the discernment to know which burdens are worth bearing and which are not.

Spiritual fitness is not gained by starving the soul through denial of our human needs. The overweight clergyman is actually suffering from malnutrition of the kind of nourishment needed to fulfill emotional needs, to satisfy deep desires, and to reward the giving of one's life in service to others. Proper nourishment of the inner self fulfills needs while also creating healthy appetite! When Jesus promised 'Blessed are those who hunger and thirst for righteousness, for they will be filled' (Matthew 5:6) it is the hunger for that which truly fulfills that receives the blessing, not a filling which quenches the thirst and kills the appetite. Healthy self-care is marked by a healthy appetite for nourishing love and healing grace.

7

Recovering from Moral Injuries to the Self

When Kevin (not his real name) came to me for pastoral counseling his complaint was that he had an unresolved problem with his father which seriously affected his ability to concentrate on his studies. He was a doctoral student at a nearby university. His doctoral research was in the area of family systems theory, and part of his assignment was to develop a comprehensive family genogram. This involved interviewing all of his immediate family members and identifying the role of each person in his family of origin.

In this process he had to deal again with the fact that he was a victim of sexual abuse by his father from the age of 8 through 13 years. The abuse stopped when his father divorced his mother, and he lived with his mother and her brother through his high school years. He had never confronted his father with this abuse, although his mother had acknowledged her awareness of it but told him that it was something that should now be forgotten. During his research, he had confronted his father. His father denied it and became very angry, accusing him of attempting to destroy his reputation and his relationship with his second wife.

'How can I recover from the damage done to me by my father if he will not acknowledge what he did? I cannot just pretend that it never happened. The other members of my family are now angry at me for causing such an upheaval over something that happened so many years ago. Am I being vindictive in attempting to get him to face up to what he did?'

'Are you angry at what he did to you then or at his refusal to accept responsibility for it now?'

'How can I tell,' he responded. It was not really a question. 'I never really felt angry about it until now. I just felt shamed. I have always thought that I must have encouraged it or he would have stopped. I understand now that he was a very sick person to do that and that I was a helpless victim. But I still feel a sense of shame in talking about it. And my anger is so strong that it is destroying me.'

As we probed his feelings of anger over a period of time, Kevin began to use words like 'I feel so violated,' 'I feel that he should pay for what he has done,' 'Why should he be allowed to live as if he has done nothing wrong?' These phrases revealed an underlying sense of moral outrage. Kevin was not only physically abused, he was violated in the most profound moral sense of the word.

The injury of moral abuse

An adolescent boy has no criteria by which he can become the moral judge of his own father. Those moral feelings of outrage had to be suppressed under a blanket of shame. The injury incurred went far deeper than emotional pain. Moral wounds to the self do not just heal over time; they must be expressed, acknowledged, and authenticated.

Feelings may be repressed but not forgotten. We can block the incident from our memory but we cannot erase the feeling it aroused in the self. This is why we are so often troubled by feelings that are experienced as keenly as when first aroused but which have become detached from the original incident or event in our minds.

Feelings which have been repressed do not gradually disappear or diminish. Emotions do not mature in the way our thinking does. When the incidents which we have blocked from our memory reappear, as in the case with Kevin, the original feelings are revived. His anger is not only against his father's denial of the earlier incidents of abuse; it is fueled by the feelings of moral outrage which he experienced through the abuse, but which were denied expression.

How can a child act as the moral judge of his own caregiver? The child is faced with a terrible dilemma. Dependent on the caregiver for physical as well as emotional support, the child represses these feelings of outrage in order to receive affection and support in other areas. The child is caught in a double bind. The person from whom the child receives the care necessary to survive also inflicts upon the child psychological and moral torment. The feelings of outrage are split off and buried within the self. This enables the mind to block out the incidents from recall, leaving blank spaces in the adult's later memory of those years.

Abuse produces moral outrage

When violations of the moral integrity of the self occur through abusive relationship with others, the injury suffered produces an outrage which can only be healed through a process of moral clarification. This involves recovery of the feelings of moral outrage and assignment of moral judgment against the offender. This is particularly difficult when the injury to the self occurred through the actions of one on whom the self was dependent for emotional and physical care and support.

The psychotherapist William Meissner (1987), says:

> We violate children and arouse them to an inner rage when we keep them from the guidance and support they need to develop fully... Moral rules are based on a primitive level of development. They are derived from fear, a response to threats of abandonment, punishment, exposure, or the inner threat of guilt, shame, or isolation. Ethical rules, however, are based on ideals to be striven for... There is a violence inherent in the moral sense. (pp.249, 252)

This violation of the self produces a reaction which he calls a primitive level of moral injury. The feeling of being shamed, abandoned, or deprived of self-pleasure, lies behind the emotion of anger and can lead to violence as an expression of the moral outrage. Later in life, these feelings of moral outrage can often lead to domestic violence on the part of the victim if healing does not occur.

The anger which Kevin now feels against his father is an expression of the moral outrage which he experienced as a child. Feelings are timeless in the sense that they are not lodged in events but in the core of the self. We plot incidents and events on a chronological continuum of past, present, and future. Feelings which are caused by incidents which occur in time become detached from this time sequence and are carried by the self in a timeless capsule.

As an adult, Kevin now recalls the incidents, and experiences the feelings as sharply and intensely as when first produced by the abusive incidents. The feeling of violation can now be acknowledged and must be dealt with as a moral issue which demands justice.

Demand for a moral verdict

Once moral outrage has been aroused, a moral verdict must be rendered. 'It's not fair,' a child will protest, when told that the trip to the amusement park has been called off. 'You promised!'

'I know I promised,' the parent responds patiently, 'but Daddy has to work this weekend and we will have to go another time.'

The parent has a good reason. Very few promises in life are unconditional. For the child, however, the moral outrage continues unabated. No verdict can be rendered which will prove satisfactory to the child. Despite all of the protest, accompanied by coercive tactics learned in other disputes, the child will lose this one. Failing to win a verdict which will appease the feeling of moral injustice, the child will often resort to punishment of the offending parent. Perhaps the parent can be made to feel guilty for failing to follow through on the promise. A prominent display of hurt feelings and a calculated period of sulking should arouse feelings of guilt in the parent, if not sympathy. Without their realizing it, the family room becomes a court room where parents are put on trial by their offspring. When the punishment has been sufficient, the child withdraws the complaint and justice has been served. Until next time!

In the case of a victim of domestic violence or child abuse, there is a deep-seated moral offense which has been committed against the person abused. The victim will need to be supported and affirmed in making a judgment against the offense as well as against the offender. The moral issue can often lie hidden in the pain caused by the abuse. Once this judgment has been rendered as rightfully directed against the offender, the victim no longer is caught in self-blame. The feelings of outrage have now been dealt with. The feelings of anger can be allowed to be processed as emotion.

Outrage is grounded in a moral sense while anger is primarily an emotion which is capable of cognitive reframing. Bringing forth a judgment against an offender draws the outrage to a conclusion. The need to punish an offender in order to satisfy moral outrage is a common feeling. But it is not the way to recovery. The moral demand is for a verdict, a judgment against the offender which satisfies the moral self. This verdict is rendered based on the facts and is supported by the moral wisdom of others who provide an objective point of reference. As in any court of law, the verdict rendered does not depend upon an admission of guilt but upon the weight of evidence submitted.

In Kevin's case, the injury done to him by his father's abuse was so deep and pervasive that the moral outrage it caused remained hidden and repressed. Lacking the resources and support to mount a moral verdict against his father, Kevin turned the judgment upon himself and felt shame rather than outrage. Unable to think of his father as an evil person, he thought of himself as a bad person. Shame is self-inflicted punishment for a perceived moral failure.

The process of recovery

The process of recovery began with the moral clarification of Kevin's anger. When he was allowed to express his anger as moral outrage against his father for the abuse, a verdict was now possible. His case was finally being brought to trial, as it were. I encouraged him to present his case as though he were the prosecuting attorney with the understanding that a verdict would be rendered.

It was a painful process. It was not easy for him to recall the specific occasions of the abuse. Details were lacking, though incidents and feelings were recoverable. He wrote out his indictment. It was almost more than he could bear. His emotions were like a roller coaster. More than once he was tempted to turn back from this exercise as it was too painful. In the end, he made his case and I, sitting as a judge, could affirm the verdict. His father was guilty as charged.

'But my father continues to deny it,' he protested. 'How can this be resolved as long as he will not admit that what he did was wrong?'

'Does his denial mean that he is not guilty?'

'I guess not,' Kevin responded. 'But I thought that I could only be healed through some kind of reconciliation with him. That's not going to happen.'

This was the crucial point in his journey to recovery. Kevin wanted his father to confess and assume responsibility as a way of making up for the injury caused. When we have been violated by another, we want the other to suffer, too, as a kind of retribution. We expect the one who has abused and shamed us to remove the shame and make right the wrong. But this is impossible. This actually allows the other the power to continue the abuse by resisting admission of guilt. Kevin did not want reconciliation as much as he wanted to punish his father as a way of removing the stigma and stain from his own life.

Once judgment has been rendered, the moral issue has been resolved and the basis for outrage removed. Anger, of course, continues, as do the feelings that the offender should suffer for the wrong done. Forgiveness does not excuse the wrongdoing nor bypass judgment. Forgiveness is only possible when the moral judgment has been rendered and supported. Forgiveness is itself a moral and spiritual achievement when it can be exercised. It is an acknowledgment that justice has been rendered through the moral judgment made and moves the self toward recovery through the building of positive self-esteem. Kevin thought that by forgiving his father he would be absolving him of the wrong. Now that a verdict has been rendered, he can begin the process of forgiving.

The moral power of forgiveness

When we find it difficult to forgive, we should search for unresolved moral outrage. The key to unlocking the power of forgiveness is the difference between a verdict, or judgment, which assigns guilt, and punishment which is meted out to the one found guilty. Forgiveness has only to do with punishment, not a judgment or verdict of guilt or innocence. Let us see why this is so.

As with Kevin, injury to the self produced an instinctive moral judgment – his own father had violated him. Along with the moral judgment there is the desire to inflict punishment against the offender. A distinction between judgment and punishment is essential in order to understand the role of forgiveness in self-recovery. A judgment is something like a verdict rendered in a court of law. One is pronounced guilty or innocent. Punishment is like the sentence imposed by the court. In determining punishment, extenuating circumstances can be taken into consideration, so that not all who are judged as guilty experience the same punishment.

Judgment and punishment can sometimes become blurred in the feelings of the victim. Moral outrage and anger are not clearly distinguished at the emotional level. Judgment and punishment are actually part of a two-step process. To judge another who has abused you as morally wrong is to satisfy the moral instinct of the self. To inflict punishment is a step beyond judgment. Punishing an offender for a wrong done may often be beyond the power or competence of the victim.

Forgiveness is not absolving an offender from judgment but is a release of the offender from punishment. For example, a good friend may betray you by sharing some information given in confidence with the result that you suffer shame and humiliation. The act of betrayal is a violation which produces an instinctive moral judgment against the one who committed the offense. If the friend, when confronted with the fact, acknowledges that betrayal indeed took place, then the issue of judgment has been resolved. Forgiveness is now possible because judgment has been rendered and the offense to the moral instinct of the self has been resolved. Releasing the offender from further punishment is what forgiveness does.

The premature demand for forgiveness

To place the burden of forgiveness upon one who has suffered moral injury to the self is often premature and unhelpful. James Leehan (1989) reminds us that it may be inappropriate to expect the moral behavior of forgiveness from the victim of abuse. The moral virtue of forgiveness offered to an offender requires an assignment of guilt as a moral context for forgiveness, which is not always present. In the case of child abuse, for example, victims of such trauma may be expected to express forgiveness as a moral or religious virtue. 'To expect forgiveness to be their initial response to abusive parents is to deny the reality of what was done to them. They need to deal with that reality in order to heal the scars which mar their lives. To berate them for their behavior may well convince them that they are not able to live up to the moral expectations or religious beliefs of any church or synagogue' (p.90).

When we have not been empowered to render judgments fairly and accurately, we tend to resort to punishment in order to compensate for the hurt we have suffered. Unfortunately, punishing others or ourselves never really satisfies the moral offense and never produces healing for the injured self. We cannot forgive ourselves or others until judgment has been fairly rendered. But we cannot do this without assistance and affirmation. Empowerment of the self must come from a source outside the self.

The Bible does not prohibit us from passing judgment against moral wrong. At the same time, it warns us about exacting vengeance against the offender. 'Beloved, never avenge yourselves,' writes the Apostle Paul, 'but leave room for the wrath of God; for it is written, "Vengeance is mine, I will repay, says the Lord"' (Romans 12:19; Deuteronomy 32:35).

Once judgment has been rendered, the moral issue has been resolved and the basis for outrage removed. Anger, of course, continues, as do the feelings that the offender should suffer for the wrong done. Forgiveness does not excuse the wrongdoing nor bypass judgment. Forgiveness is only possible when the moral judgment has been rendered and supported. Forgiveness is itself a moral and spiritual achievement when it can be exercised. It is an acknowledgment that justice has been rendered through the moral judgment made and moves the self toward recovery by releasing the moral power of forgiveness.

When the abuse is denied

Suppose the offender in the case of abuse denies the offense, as happened in Kevin's case. When an offender does not acknowledge the wrong done through abuse, it is difficult, if not impossible, for forgiveness to be expressed. This is because forgiveness demands a moral threshold upon which to stand, ordinarily established when a judgment has been rendered. Behind all injuries to the self, regardless of the cause, there is a moral need for justice to be done. This can take the form of expressing a moral judgment on behalf of the injured person, even if the offender will not acknowledge responsibility.

In the case of Kevin, his father denied that he had sexually abused his son, though it had been acknowledged by his mother. As I worked through the process of seeking a verdict with him, he began to see his father as really guilty of a crime against him. His feelings of having been violated were now affirmed as having moral validity. Reconciliation with his father would not be possible until his father accepted responsibility and offered repentance.

When we discussed what punishment should now be brought against his father, Kevin began to have different feelings than he had before. 'I have no desire to hurt my father,' said Kevin. 'I feel sorry for him. He must feel miserable inside knowing what he did but not being able to face it.'

'Does this mean that you have no need nor desire to punish him?' I asked.

He was quiet for a long time, but then said, 'There is nothing to be gained by punishing him now. If forgiveness means that I still feel he is guilty but that I have no need nor desire to punish him, then, yes, I can forgive him.'

Can we forgive the unforgivable?

What are we to say to those who remind us that some who commit acts of outrageous evil ought never to be forgiven? Simon Wiesenthal tells of an incident while he was in a Polish concentration camp. A nurse took him to the bed of a dying SS Nazi, 22 years old. The soldier, whose name was Karl, said he had to speak to a Jew, to confess his crime of murdering innocent women and children. He begged Wiesenthal, as a Jew, to forgive him so that he could die in peace. Wiesenthal said, 'I stood up and looked in his direction, at his folded hands. At last I made up my mind and without a word I left the room.' The German went to God unforgiven by man. Later, a fellow prisoner wrote, 'You would have had no right to forgive him in the name of people who had not authorized you to do so. What people have done to you, yourself, you can, if you like, forgive and forget. That is your affair. But it would have been a terrible sin to burden your conscience with other people's suffering' (Smedes 1984, p.127).

Lewis Smedes (1984) is not entirely comfortable with a concept of evil which frees us from the responsibility of forgiveness. In his own commentary on this story, he wrote:

> Forgiving does not reduce evil. Forgiving great evil does not shave a millimeter from its monstrous size. There is no real forgiving unless there is first relentless exposure and honest judgment. When we forgive evil we do not excuse it, we do not tolerate it, we do not smother it. We look the evil full in the face, call it what it is. Let it's horror shock and stun and enrage us, and only then do we forgive it... When we declare an evil person to be beyond the pale of forgiveness, we create a monster who does not even *need* to be forgiven – a monster is excused from judgment by the fact that he or she is beyond humanity. This is the paradox of making any human being *absolutely* evil. (pp.79–80)

The moral power of mercy

I suspect that what Smedes calls forgiveness is really mercy. Forgiveness is not always a possibility, but mercy is. There are people who may be beyond forgiveness on human terms, but even as evil humans are not to be excluded from mercy. For in becoming merciless, we also become inhuman.

In releasing oneself from the moral mandate to punish, the offender still must face punishment for violating a moral law. It is not as though forgiveness exempts the offender from further punishment. Rather, forgiveness only has to do with the relation of the victim to the offender, not of the offender to the moral law. It is the responsibility of the community, or the State, to provide appropriate punishment where a crime has been committed. Even then, punishment must take into account the moral demand of mercy.

In showing mercy, one seeks to alleviate pain, temper justice, and restore relationships. While mercy is prompted by compassion, it has its source in the moral virtue of promoting the value of a human life when it least deserves it or cannot bear it. We applaud acts of mercy because we recognize the moral goodness of such actions which go beyond the legal demands of the law.

While some people show no mercy because they have no compassion, others who have deep feelings of compassion are reluctant to extend mercy in fear of undermining justice. Punishment for violation of either a natural, civil, or divine law contains the moral content of the law itself. This is not the responsibility of the victim but of the community and society to which the victim belongs.

The moral value of mercy as the basis for forgiveness is grounded in the moral being of God and of humans created in the divine image. Forgiveness has to do with release from punishment on the part of the victim, not exemption from the law. Mercy is shown to those who have no power or right to establish their own righteousness and human well-being. Mercy is a moral demand while forgiveness is not. We cannot hold persons accountable to forgive when they have been sinned against, but we can expect them to show mercy where it is appropriate. Where forgiveness is offered, mercy has preceded it and constitutes the moral basis for forgiving. For example, when Kevin came to the place where he could free his father from further punishment, he was showing mercy, and was then morally empowered to forgive.

The spiritual freedom of forgiveness

To release oneself from the moral demand for punishment against another for an offense against one's own life is to free oneself, to discover a power which expands the horizons of self-awareness beyond all the given boundaries and burdens. Jesus gave the key: 'Whatever you loose on earth will be loosed in heaven' (Matthew 16:19). To discover the inner resources to forgive another of an offense against one's life is to experience a spiritual power and freedom which stops the hurting and starts the healing.

Not all of us have been abused and not many of us awakened in life to discover that we had a crippling or disfiguring birth defect. But all of us know what moral outrage is and what it is like to feel a victim of unfairness, regardless of the source. From our first experience of life we experience injuries to the self and reach out for healing.

Moral advocacy for the victim

Those who have been the victims of abusive behavior need an advocate to enter in and empower the person offended to render a moral judgment against the offender, whether the offender acknowledges wrong or not. This intervention serves to authenticate the outrage done to the self and serves to render a moral judgment against the offender and on behalf of the victim. This does make forgiveness possible in the sense of giving over to God the punishment (vengeance) and freeing the self to be healed of the hurt and anger.

Forgiveness and reconciliation are a social as well as a spiritual reality which must be pursued for the sake of our own healing and recovery. 'If another member of the church sins against you,' said Jesus, 'go and point out the fault when the two of you are alone. If the member listens to you, you have regained that one' (Matthew 18:15). The Mennonite theologian, Norman Kraus (1987), argues that reconciliation between humans and God through Christ is a social act as well as a forensic one.

The intention of forgiveness is to nullify shame and guilt so that reconciliation and a new beginning become possible. The shamed person must find new identity and personal worth. And the guilty person must find expiation. Both objective alienation and hostility which have been institutionalized in our social and legal systems and the subjective remorse and blame that so inhibit personal fulfillment in human relationships must be overcome... Only a forgiveness which covers the past and a genuine restoration of relationship can banish shame. What is needed is a restoration of communication. The rage which isolates and insulates must be overcome. Reconciliation and restoration of mutual intimate relationship through a loving open exchange is the only way to heal resentment and restore lost self-esteem. (pp.207, 211)

Forgiveness must not be content with 'forgetting the past,' but must acknowledge and transform our memory of the past. David Augsburger (1988) comments that for many who appear to have forgotten the past, their 'memory just became fatigued – which is not true forgiveness!' (p. 48).

The journey toward forgiveness and healing

Forgiveness is a journey, sometimes a life-long journey. We have no control over the end – some relationships can and will never be mended this side of heaven. Some offenses are so grievous that it is not within our power to forgive. And yet the journey must begin, for it is a journey toward our own freedom and peace. Augsburger (1988) says:

Forgiveness is not an act – it is a process. It is not a single transaction – it is a series of steps. Beware of any view of instant, complete, once-for-all forgiveness. Instant solutions tend to be the ways of escape, of avoidance, or of denial, not of forgiveness. Forgiveness takes time – time to be aware of one's feelings, alert to one's pain and anger, open to understand the other's perspective, willing to resolve the pain and reopen the future. (p.42)

Healing the pain

Each of us has pain in our lives, whether it be chronic physical pain, the emotional pain of unhealed grief, or the pain of unfulfilled desires and dreams. Whatever the cause of pain, the cry of pain is the same. We cannot really hear the pain of others until we can speak with a voice that pain recognizes. At the same time, as Elaine Scarry (1985) reminds us, there really is no language for pain. The 'cry of pain' is not mute, but neither is it articulate. We cannot really 'listen to pain,' we can only share pain.

We only begin to trust one who can share our pain. The sympathy of those who recognize our hurt and wish to help is not sufficient. Those who are vulnerable at the level of their own pain create access to our pain, and thus to the very core of our being, without requiring a commitment or a promise. With the experience of shared pain, those whose trust has been shattered can find a point of beginning.

Further, the reality of shared pain creates an implicit bond which requires explicit recognition and affirmation. Once we have experienced bonding through shared pain, there is a further step now possible. The implicit bond of companionship and shared life has now taken the place of the distrust which served as a protective mechanism against risking further hurt. While there is not yet a capacity to make promises that require trust, there is 'moral ground under one's feet,' so to speak. The ones who provided unconditional acceptance through their own shared pain now stand with us and for us. There is less risk involved in saying 'yes' to the reality of a bond already established than the attempt to create a new one 'out of nothing.' This is the therapeutic role of the community of faith as the gracious and healing presence of God's love and Spirit.

Moral injuries to the self are not healed as are other injuries. Rather, these injuries must be treated as violations of one's innate sense of moral dignity and personhood. Recovery begins when a moral verdict is rendered in one's favor. This is impossible for the morally wounded self to do alone. The recovery of moral health results from the uncovering of the moral abuse and the discovery of moral empowerment.

Moral empowerment for recovery

The uncovering of moral abuse as the basis of moral outrage requires moral support. This requires sensitivity to the injury sustained through a violation of the self's innate dignity of personhood. A perception of moral injury is an insight beyond that of a diagnosis of emotional pain. With this insight, the one who provides moral support and clarification leads the injured one through a process resulting in a moral judgment against the offender. This process uncovers the source of the moral outrage and directs the moral judgment away from the victim toward the offender. This is the process which enabled Kevin to release his moral outrage against his father for the abuse he suffered as a child.

The discovery of moral empowerment is a second phase of the recovery process. Moral outrage which fails to be expressed honestly and accurately against the offender is deflected back upon the victim as shame and self-condemnation. Shame is a loss of moral worth and power. The power of shame is secrecy. As long as we keep the secret of our violation and abuse to ourselves, we feel safe and protected. The power of shame is only broken when we are empowered by a new sense of moral and personal worth. When Kevin began to experience the moral freedom to judge his father's actions as wrong, he discovered the moral depths of his outrage.

Moral outrage, after all, is a moral expression of the self. When it is repressed, the moral core becomes split off and turns an accusing eye upon the self, producing shame and self-condemnation. When moral outrage is expressed as anger it becomes destructive and even violent. The discovery of moral empowerment results from the discovery of the true moral self as endowed with the divine image and likeness.

The biblical story of Adam and Eve reveals the source of moral empowerment as they are confronted by their Creator following their fall from grace (Genesis 2, 3). Led astray by the serpent, who covered his evil intention with the pretense of good, Adam and Eve lost their innocent and trusting relationship with each other. They now felt shame and self-condemnation. They covered themselves with fig leaves and hid themselves in the garden from the presence of God.

Confronted by God, they complain that they were tricked by the serpent, an acknowledgment of their own failure as much as an indictment of the evil one. The first judgment of God is against the serpent, who is brought under a curse for leading astray two of God's children. Two things then take place with regard to Adam and Eve. They are forced to lay aside the fig leaves which cover their shame, and then are clothed by God with the skins of animals.

These are powerful metaphors. As God's children, Adam and Eve are endowed with the divine image and likeness which is an innate sense of moral worth and value. As they are open and supportive of each other's integrity and worth, they story says that they were 'both naked, and were not ashamed.' When they experience the violation of that inner sense of value through the misleading guidance of the serpent, there is no open expression of moral outrage. Rather, this outrage is deflected back upon themselves and the moral injury they receive drives them into secrecy.

Spiritual empowerment for recovery

With the skill of a moral surgeon, God uncovers their sense of shame and moral confusion. There is no curse directed at the couple. Rather, the serpent receives the full force of the divine moral outrage as the one who has seduced and violated the children. While there are consequences of their actions which each must accept, the moral judgment of God turns into moral empowerment. They receive more than mercy. The metaphor of clothing which God provides is a gracious sign that they are accepted and valued as the children of God that they essentially are.

Did the serpent ever confess and acknowledge his moral crime against God's children? Never! But the verdict has been rendered. God serves notice. His moral outrage against the offender is the source of divine compassion and mercy directed toward those who bear his image, and the source of judgment and retribution toward those who violate that human image and likeness.

Central to the biblical story and the Judeo-Christian tradition is the reality of God as the defender of the defenseless and one who hears the cries of the oppressed. When we understand that each person has been endowed with the image and likeness of God, we can hear the outrage of those who are violated as an expression of a divine moral outrage. The God of Israel is a God who takes up the cause of those who have suffered at the hands of others and who asserts the moral worth and value of those who have suffered moral injustice.

While the prophets pronounce judgment against those who oppress others and fail to show mercy and love, their underlying theme is the moral verdict which God renders on behalf of those who have become victims.

> Justice is turned back, and righteousness stands at a distance; for truth stumbles in the public square, and uprightness cannot enter. Truth is lacking, and whoever turns from evil is despoiled. The Lord saw it, and it displeased him that there was no justice. He saw that there was no one, and was appalled that there was no one to intervene; so his own arm

brought him victory and his righteousness upheld him. (Isaiah 59:14–16)

Jesus issued a stern warning against those who violate the moral dignity and value of those whom God cares for. 'Take care that you do not despise one of these little ones; for, I tell you, in heaven their angels continually see the face of my Father in heaven' (Matthew 18:10).

But where really do we find the ultimate source of empowerment when our moral selves have been wounded and we need a moral verdict rendered on our behalf rather than moral judgment? To whom can we turn when we feel forsaken and abandoned, without a moral advocate and devastated by our own sense of failure and shame? For many, the religious community provides a source of empowering love, including priests and pastors who mediate the grace and healing power of God. Therapists and counselors provide psychological assistance for the process of healing and recovery of emotional and mental health. Recovery groups and 12-step programs offer a process and context of healing and growth. The beginning step of authentic recovery is the moral and spiritual empowerment that only God can give. Recovery does not come though the healing of emotional pain alone. True recovery means the discovery of one's own moral and spiritual self as affirmed by God and empowered through divine love and grace.

8

Casting Light on the Dark Side of Human Spirituality

She was a young woman in her early twenties. She walked into my office for her first appointment carrying the largest Bible I had ever seen. She sat down, holding this enormous Bible against her chest with both hands wrapped around it as though it were either a shield to ward off enemy spears or a life-jacket to save her own life from drowning. It was probably the latter, though I suspect that it served more like an anchor dragging her under than a life-preserver.

She had been referred to me by a psychologist, who asked me to see her as he had been unable to discover her problem and help her despite several months of therapy. In addition, she no longer could afford paying for mental health services and her therapist asked me, a pastoral counselor, to give her whatever help I could.

I discovered that she had also been bringing the Bible to her sessions with the psychotherapist in the same compulsive way. She related to me her background in a fundamentalist church where she was taught that the human self was intrinsically bad and only through the implanting of a new, spiritual self could she please God.

Week after week, the woman came, clutching the same Bible, her grasp on it becoming more compulsive each time she came close to naming the terror that tormented her. She would sometimes sit for several minutes, hunched over the Bible, unable to speak. At times, when she did finally speak, she would appear to undergo a personality change, emoting anger and with a terrified look in her eyes. On one occasion, after lashing out at God in a verbal tirade, she looked at a cross which was hanging on my wall and said, 'As for Jesus, I don't think that he ever existed. No one has seen him, and I think that the church has made him up.'

I quietly replied, 'The only Jesus that you will ever see is sitting here in this room with you.' At that, she threw her Bible down on the floor and began to stomp around the room hurling curses and obscenities at everyone and no one in particular. When she finally calmed down I told her to sit down. I took her hand and, looking into her eyes, I said, 'I can pray for you and you can be healed of that terrible thing which causes you to do this.' As I prayed, not breaking eye contact, she began to weep and her face softened.

After a few moments she said, 'I have been a terrible person and have done terrible things. I think that the devil got into me. Is God going to kill me for that?'

'What do you think?' I responded.

For a long while she looked at me. Then she said, 'No, I guess not. So what do we do now?' She picked up the Bible which still lay on the floor and laid it in her lap, folding her hands on top.

'My pastor once told me that I was possessed of a demon,' she said. 'Several men of the church laid hands on my head and prayed for me to be delivered from the demon and from the power of Satan. When nothing happened, I left the church and have never been back. Did I really have a demon and did your prayer drive it out of me?'

I was quite unprepared to answer her question, both theologically and pastorally. As it turned out, she did not pursue the issue and we proceeded with therapy.

The demonic and mental illness

My preparation for ministry in a theological seminary did not include a theology of demons nor a practical theology of deliverance from demonic possession. It did not occur to me in the session with the young woman that her bizarre behavior was caused by a demon. I simply felt compassion for her and prayed for her healing with an emphasis not on the source of the evil power causing her to act in this way but on the reality of God's power and peace which was even then flowing into her life.

What seemed important to me at the time was that she trusted that I would not condemn or judge her, allowing her to share some of the terrible things which she had done. Thus I instinctively maintained eye contact with her so that she would not feel isolated and abandoned, even in being prayed for. I did not want her to feel merely an object of prayer, but a truly valuable person in my eyes and in God's eyes.

As we worked together on her emotional and mental health she disclosed a severely distorted and conflicted self-concept in which her view of God as an angry and condemning judge was predominant. She began to ask 'what God would think,' or 'what God would say' about certain aspects of her self-disclosure.

In reflecting on this case, I began to see two things. First, the psychotherapist who had been working with her dealt primarily with her feelings of shame, lack of self-worth, and emotional pain. His diagnosis, as reported to me in the referral, was some form of obsessive–compulsive disorder. Not being a trained psychotherapist, I had no competence to continue that line of therapy. At the same time, I attempted to let her reveal her feelings and talk about the kind of compulsive behavior that was causing problems in her daily life without diagnostic intervention. I also ignored the Bible which she clutched in her hands and made no attempt to question her about it even when she revealed thoughts and behavior which a pastor might well consider inconsistent with a biblical pattern of life.

The use of Scripture

As she progressed in her recovery, I would often select certain texts from Scripture related to her sense of self and ask her to tell me what she thought the Word of God was saying to her. I sought by this means to awaken in her a response, or 'hearing,' of the Word of God, not merely to 'tell' her what the Bible said. The critical turning point came when she was able to acknowledge the thing which finally came to the surface as something that God might 'kill her for.'

The second thing which I came to understand is that she viewed me as not only a counselor but as someone who represented God because of my connection with the church and my pastoral role. In what might seem a paradox, she was only able to acknowledge the source of her problem as having spiritual ramifications in the context where God's presence was recognized. Rather than a secular psychotherapist providing a 'safe' place for her, it was the absence of a spiritual dimension in that relationship which prevented her healing and recovery.

The nature of the human person has been described in the beginning of this book as an integrative gestalt, where the social, personal, sexual, and psychical components of the self are grounded in the spiritual. The mental and physical dimensions of the self impinge upon each of these. When there is some degree of disassociation between these elements, the sexual and personal, or personal and social, for instance, the self is thrown off balance and subject to impersonal forces within competing for attention and used for self-gratification. In the case of this young woman, she had some rather intense religious formation of the self but at the expense of her personal self-identity. Rather than her religious foundation serving as a source of spiritual empowerment, it deviated into an obsessive–compulsive pattern of life. What she needed was a more authentic spirituality which began with her social, personal and sexual reorientation and integration. When we consider spiritual resources for emotional and mental health, we must look more deeply into our own relationship with God. We need competence in hearing the voice of the human spirit as well as of the human psyche.

Spirituality and religiosity

The spiritual core of the human self is not intrinsically religious. Religious dimensions of spirituality emerge as the self engages and is encountered by the Spirit of God. When the human spirit becomes autonomous, not directed by or toward the Spirit of God, a dark side of spirituality emerges which can take the form of self-destructive thoughts, actions, and behavior. Out of this dark spirituality comes what the Apostle Paul calls works of the flesh: 'fornication, impurity, licentiousness, idolatry, sorcery, enmities, strife, jealousy, anger, quarrels, dissensions, factions, envy, drunkenness, carousing, and things like these' (Galatians 5:19–21).

Paul suggests that those whose spiritual life is not directed by God's Spirit are abandoned to lives which represent every form of inhumanity: 'God gave them up to a debased mind and to things that should not be done. They were filled with every kind of wickedness, evil, covetousness, malice. Full of envy, murder, strife, deceit, craftiness, they are gossips, slanderers, God-haters, insolent, haughty, boastful, inventors of evil, rebellious toward parents, foolish, faithless, heartless, ruthless' (Romans 1:28–31). An even more desperate picture of those who are bereft of divine spiritual presence is presented by Jude: 'They are waterless clouds carried along by the winds; autumn trees without fruit, twice dead, uprooted; wild waves of the sea, casting up the foam of their own shame;

wandering stars, for whom the deepest darkness has been reserved forever' (Jude 1:12,13).

In this view, human spirituality is never neutral and therefore liable to distortion and even demonic manifestations of inhuman and anti-human behavior. Not all spirituality is good. Some forms of spirituality are dark and dangerous. The concept of evil has challenged philosophers, theologians, and psychologists over the centuries. In his helpful survey of the various responses to the problem of evil, Dominic Walker (2002) concludes that if there were a solution to the problem of evil and human suffering we would solve the riddle of life itself. Beyond the problem of evil, however, is the existence of a world of demonic spirits which oppress and torment the human spirit.

What I am left with, even now, is the unsettling and difficult question as to what to make of the matter of demonic possession and exorcism. There is unmistakable evidence of a dark side to human spirituality. Psychologists have names for the various disorders which appear as personality disturbances, but they do not ordinarily include the concept of evil, much less demonic possession. My concern in this chapter is to examine this dark side from the perspective of practical theology, hoping to provide some guidance, if not answers to questions which arise among mental health caregivers.

A case of dark spirituality

Deborah van Deusen Hunsinger (1995), a Jungian trained psychotherapist and Professor of Pastoral Theology at Princeton Theological Seminary, in her book *Theology & Pastoral Counseling*, discusses the case of 'Eva and Her "black Despairs."' As Hunsinger describes the case, Eva experienced intense periods of what she called 'black despair.' She was convinced that God was offended at this and heaped scorn upon herself for not being able to 'pull herself out of it.' She chose a pastoral counselor because she felt that she needed spiritual guidance as well as psychological help. At one point in the therapy process, Eva began to externalize 'voices' which were destructive to her self-image and savage in tone, leaving her with self-hatred and contempt. At this point, Hunsinger suggested that the voices might be 'demonic.' Up to this point, Eva had internalized these voices as those of her parents, whom she also identified as 'God-like' figures. By attributing a demonic quality to the 'voices' Hunsinger challenged the 'divine' authority which the voices appeared to have. As a result, Eva began to work creatively with this interpretation. Hunsinger (1995) describes it in this way, drawing upon the biblical account of the man possessed by demons (Luke 8:26–39) (pp.151–212).

> Eva, like the demoniac, lived among the dead. Her mother, nearly twenty years in the grave, was a daily companion, and Eva's fear of the imminent deaths of her father and sister haunted her continually. During her depressive episodes, Eva, like the demoniac, seemed to be wandering among the tombs, cut off from her fellow human beings and from all sense of hope. She, too, inflicted great harm on herself, crying aloud day and night, filled with alien, destructive energies over which she had no control. She, too, need to be liberated from the abusive forces that inhabited her very being. (p.163)

Hunsinger's therapeutic approach combined psychodynamic interpretation and intervention with spiritual guidance. She came alongside Eva to challenge the evil forces in her with an arsenal of spiritual weapons: truth, righteousness, peace, faith, salvation, the Word of God, and prayer (Ephesians 6:10–18a). This process took months, but in the end, Hunsinger reports,

> as we prayed together at the close of the session, an image of Jesus driving the money changers from the temple came to Eva's mind. She, Eva, was God's temple and the Lord was consumed with zeal for the Lord's house... The feeling of an imminent depressive episode, which had been intensifying with the usual manifestations was suddenly ameliorated. Eva did not fall into one of her black despairs but was dramatically delivered from it. (p.171)

In retrospect, Hunsinger acknowledges that both she and Eva were using the concept of 'demonic voices' loosely and metaphorically. She concludes, 'Although literal "exorcism" seemed to be neither palatable nor particularly pertinent, Eva and I did approach the signs of her "possession" from a standpoint of faith... Eva prayed, at times, fervently, for Christ to cast out the demons that so oppressed her' (p.207).

Are we engaged in spiritual warfare?

If Hunsinger leaves us uncertain as to what is meant by demonic possession and whether or not in speaking of demons we are treating psychotic disorder without 'naming the devil,' others are more explicit. A cultural anthropologist and missiologist, Charles Kraft (1992) makes it quite clear that a great deal of emotional trauma and mental disorders are caused by demons that invade the human personality. In his book, *Defeating Dark Angels*, he describes case after case where liberation from demonic oppression results from a therapeutic approach called 'deep healing.' Kraft not only has written about demonic possession he also practices various levels of liberation through a personal ministry of healing and liberation.

Church growth specialist C. Peter Wagner has written widely about the phenomenon of demonic power both at the personal and social level. He now heads an organization devoted to an international ministry of prayer focused specifically on challenging the 'territorial demonic spirits' in order to free cities and their population from demonic oppression. Wagner (1992, 1993) argues that social transformation and liberation from demonic political power structures can take place by challenging the evil powers which hold humans in bondage. New Testament scholar Robert Guelich (1991), on the other hand, argues that the concept of spiritual warfare is largely absent from the New Testament. He suggests that the warfare language used by the Apostle Paul, for example, should be understood metaphorically rather than literally (for example, Ephesians 6:10–17). The victory of Jesus over evil powers ended with his death and resurrection. The battle is over. We who walk in the power of Christ's life and by his Spirit do not confront evil powers on our own, but rest in the victory of Christ. (For additional sources on spiritual warfare see Peter Horrobin 1994; Peter Lundell 2001; Jeffrey Means 2000; B.J. Oropeza 1997; George Otis 1997; John Thomas 1998; Walter Wink 1986, 1992, 1998.)

WHAT ARE WE TO MAKE OF DEMONS?

'Was I possessed by a demon?' asked the young woman for whom I prayed and who experienced a rather dramatic transformation leading to a good therapeutic outcome. While she did not press me for an answer, I have been hard pressed by many others – students, pastors and professional caregivers – who encounter what only can be called evil in some persons with whom they come in contact during therapy. Do demons actually exist? Are they really 'dark angels'? Not really, says Karl Barth, but we need to listen to him carefully.

It was Karl Barth (1960b) who introduced one of the most comprehensive discussions of angels in contemporary theology. As a subcategory under his discussion of angels as God's ambassadors he discusses 'their opponents.' Rather than adopting the medieval distinction between good angels (*angeli boni*) and bad angels (*angeli mali*), Barth suggests that demons are in a category of their own. The 'bad angels' are not a special species of angels but an entity which is condemned and opposed by angels which are 'good.' He rejects what some scholars suggest, that Satan may once have been an angel that 'fell from heaven' (Isaiah 14:12). 'The devil was never an angel,' Barth assures us, not even a fallen one. Barth categorizes the demons as belonging to the 'nothingness' which stands opposed to God's creative Word and world. Angels and demons are related as creation and chaos, as good and evil, as life and death, and as the light of revelation and the darkness which will not receive it.

As a result, Barth does not attribute real 'being' to Satan or the demons in the same sense as that which God has called 'into being' through a creative Word. Even as God did not create darkness, but only light, with the darkness emerging as the shadow side of light, so God never created evil or evil beings. However, what God created as 'good being' immediately had a shadow side called 'nonbeing,' or nothingness (*das Nichtige*). Consequently, says Barth, demons do not exist as having 'real being' so that we can 'believe in demons' in the same way that we believe in the reality that God created and sustains. At the same time, Barth is quite specific about the phenomenological reality of demonic power (pp.120–128).

BUT DEMONS SHOULD NOT BE IGNORED

Barth (1958) issues a warning: 'If we ignore demons, they deceive us by concealing their power until we are again constrained to respect and fear them as powers. If we absolutise them, respecting and fearing them as true powers, they have deceived us by concealing their character as falsehood, it will be only a little while before we try to ignore and are thus deceived by them again' (pp.526–527). At the same time, Barth (1960b) cautions: 'We cannot deny that in their infamous way they are real and brisk and vital, often serious and solemn, but always sly and strong, and always present in different combinations of these qualities, forming a dreadful fifth or sixth dimension of existence.' In the end, Barth (1960b) concludes, 'The very thing which the demons are waiting for, especially in theology, is that we should find them interesting and give them our serious and perhaps systematic attention' (p.519).

The Bible does not appear concerned about the origin of evil or of Satan and the demonic world. It simply declares their existence, warns against their influence, and points toward their eventual annihilation. The most one might say is that evil is some kind of mutation from the good, if such a thing is possible. In any event, as Barth suggests, we are better not to be preoccupied with the origin and 'being' of evil, but to concentrate on the power of God's good Spirit to resist the pull toward dark spirituality and to draw us toward health and wholeness.

The distinction which Barth makes between the 'being' of demons and their 'existence' is a technical theological point meant to overcome the concept of an essential dualism between God and Satan and between good and evil. This is an important theological point, but it is also a crucial practical one. At the popular level we make little distinction between the existence of things and the 'being' of things. To say that demons 'exist' is usually considered to mean that they are real entities in the same way as other entities, angels, or supernatural beings, for instance.

When our body temperature is elevated beyond normal we often say, 'I have a fever.' Now a fever is a medical condition which affects the entire body system as well as one's mental state. Having a 'fever' affects one's state of mind, emotions, and general outlook on life. Without effective treatment, a fever can lead to death. Yet, when we wake up the following day and say, 'The fever is gone,' we ordinarily do not ask, 'Where has it gone?' At one point we name the fever and treat its existence as something alien to the health of the body system, but at another point we release the semantic hold which we have placed on the condition by naming it, and do not 'pursue' it so as to find where it has 'gone.' While this analogy fails as much as it might help, it does serve to remind us that in somewhat the same way, a demonic 'fever' may be produced as a form of spiritual disorder with real effects which cause mental illness as well as aberrant behavior. When the 'demon' is banished, by whatever means, we can understand that what we have 'named' is no longer an entity which exists as a supernatural power which we should fear as much outside the self as within. Thus, it should not be a matter of concern whether or not demons 'exist,' as though we should conduct a campaign of 'spiritual warfare' against them.

WE SHOULD NOT FOCUS ON THE DEMONIC

It becomes a more serious matter, however, when we think of a demon 'existing' within a human personality. When we think of demons in this way we internalize demons as alien, evil beings which have invaded the human self, taken up residence, and are controlling us. Once we have internalized this idea, if the demon cannot be exorcized or driven out, we are left with the terrible feeling that an evil entity remains within us. It is one thing to say, 'I believe that there are demons and that Satan is real.' It is quite another thing to believe that, 'I have a demon within me,' or, 'Satan is inside of me.'

Andrea Yates, a woman in Texas, methodically killed five of her children by drowning them in a bathtub. Psychologists diagnosed her condition as a case of severe post-partum depression following the birth of her youngest child and stated that, while she was mentally ill, she was competent to stand trial. Testimony introduced into the trial quoted her as saying that 'I am Satan and it is time for me to be punished.' She also said that if she were executed, 'Satan will die with me' (*Orange County Register,* 2001).

The horror of a woman killing her own children is too much for the human spirit to bear. Attributing such an act to Satan or to demonic possession may not only be a tactic used by a defense attorney in a trial to support a defense of incompetence due to mental illness, it may also be a way for many to account for such darkness of the human spirit.

ARE WE HELPLESS PAWNS IN THE BATTLE BETWEEN GOOD AND EVIL?

Is it possible that demonic possession can account for some extreme form of mental illness and the evil things that humans do to one another? Are we helpless pawns in a cosmic battle between good and evil? Are we so devoid of our own moral and spiritual goodness that we are dependent upon a 'good' spirit to invade and occupy us as the only alternative to being invaded and occupied by an 'evil spirit'?

Marguerite Shuster (1987) appears to concede this point. Her basic argument is that openness to the phenomenon of demonic possession is grounded in the very nature of the self and thus should be taken into account in dealing with emotional and spiritual problems. She views the human self as basically without any spiritual or moral power of its own. The self either will be controlled from without by the good Spirit and purpose of God or by the evil and malicious purpose of Satan. As a result, she comes very close to identifying all forms of suffering with some form of 'possession' by an evil spirit or spirits. It is understandable then that she should take a quite negative view of psychotherapy in favor of a form of pastoral care that treats most psychological problems as a spiritual power conflict.

The mention of evil in the context of mental illness comes close to labeling sickness itself as evil. 'Evil is a powerful interpretative label which, when ascribed to individuals, removes them from our therapeutic horizon and leaves them stranded, alienated and vulnerable to forms of treatment which are oppressive and dehumanizing' (Swinton 2002). Mental health caregivers, Swinton goes on to say, 'can themselves become perpetrators of evil.' On the other hand, if we label all evil as mental illness we might be more forgiving and less judgmental. This can make us feel better, as Gwen Adshead (2002) says, but we 'may miss a sense of agency in the actor, that is to say, his or her ownership of the evil event and it is that sense of agency that bothers people afterwards.' When mental illness is used to provide an explanation or an excuse for what is construed to be an evil act, the 'forensic patient,' to use her terminology, is not helped to deal with issues of moral and spiritual self-identity.

I want to suggest a more hopeful view of the human self with respect to casting some light on the dark side of spirituality.

Casting light on the dark side of spirituality

My own approach to the issue of demon possession as one cause of emotional and mental disorder is to say that it is sufficient to remove the effects of evil without having to name the source. The effects of evil are clearly defined in the Bible as those which violate, abuse, torment, disfigure, disorient, and destroy human life at both the personal and social level. Such evil also includes outrageous actions against God. However, it is also clear that much evil can be done in the name of God, so that religious pretense and moral self-assurance can often mask evil intentions and actions. Jesus denounces the self-righteous religious leaders who seek to discredit his ministry if not his very person by saying, 'You are from your father, the devil, and you choose to do your father's desires' (John 8:44). In response to his disciple Peter, who sought to dissuade him from going to Jerusalem in order to save his own life by invoking God's name, Jesus responded: 'Get behind me, Satan! You are a stumbling block to me; for you are setting your mind not on divine things, but on human things' (Matthew 16:23).

There is no indication that the other disciples immediately identified Peter as possessed of Satan, and no exorcism was performed! They clearly understood this as a warning not to impose their own intentions and desires upon Jesus so as to divert him from fulfilling God's intentions for his life. Again, I suggest that the focus is on the effects of evil not upon the source. When one conforms to God's will, as Peter finally did, a positive effect is evidence of spiritual guidance that leads to a good outcome, despite the suffering and even some failures along the way, as Peter also learned.

A therapy of disbelief

The young woman who came to me lived with the nagging thought that she was possessed of a demon as a result of the ritual of exorcism conducted by her church. How else was she to understand the failure of exorcism other than the fact that once a demon had been diagnosed as the cause of her problem she was left to struggle with it on her own? Part of the pastoral counsel which I was able to offer included a 'therapy of disbelief' in being demon possessed as a result of the positive growth and inner peace which she now possessed as she moved toward mental health and positive self-control.

In the case of Eva, as reported by Hunsinger (1995), the effects of evil were removed through a combination of psychotherapeutic intervention and spiritual guidance. In this case, attributing the evil to demonic voices served a therapeutic purpose in removing the effects of evil. In the end, Eva's recovery was not conditioned upon her continued 'belief in demons' but in affirming the healing and health which she received. 'Eva was God's temple and the Lord was consumed with zeal for the Lord's house' (p.171).

If, in fact, the religious ritual of exorcism is used to remove the effects of evil, then the practice should be considered as part of the overall therapeutic strategy needed to produce positive effects. In the case of the young woman I mentioned at the beginning of this chapter, the church's use of exorcism did not produce a positive effect. The woman was left in 'worse condition' than before. One can assume that those who performed the exorcism abandoned her while continuing to believe in the demons. Samuel Southard (1989) comments on the case of a woman freed from a demonic power through a psychiatrist working with an Episcopalian priest as a member of the team. Following her release from this power, the woman found a place of belonging and acceptance in a church where she said, 'I wanted to be in a place where I was accepted and I wanted to help others who were all bound up as I was' (pp.248–254). The role of the faith-community in recovery from mental illness has been documented and discussed by John Swinton (2000b).

A bilingual approach

Those who encounter persons caught in the dark side of human spirituality need discernment and wisdom in 'hearing' the different voices which come to expression in the counseling room. Every person expresses emotional and mental pain through two languages, suggests Hunsinger (1995). At one level, emotional and mental pain can only be heard through the 'ear' of psychological insight. This requires competence in 'speaking' the language of the human psyche. At another level, the same person may be expressing pain which can only be heard by one competent in the 'language of the spirit.' What she suggests is that caregivers need to be 'bilingual' so as to hear what the person in need is expressing and respond accordingly. 'The metaphor of "becoming bilingual"…suggests that pastoral counselors need to reflect more carefully on what it would mean to be proficient in two different languages, one the language of depth psychology, the other the language of faith' (p.9).

This does not mean, she goes on to suggest, that the pastoral counselor tries to 'translate' the material being expressed by the person in need from one idiom to another. 'The issues, whether theological or psychological, still function within their own linguistic frame of reference.' The issue of desire, for example, is 'not only a psychological issue but also a theological one.' So too with the use of Scripture. 'There is a difference between understanding Scripture as Word of God and understanding it as a psychologically profound book of stories and wisdom that capture some essential aspect of being human. The normative force of hearing Scripture as the Word of God is different from hearing it as possibly illustrating a significant psychological insight.' Of course, she goes on to say, Scripture may function in both ways and the pastoral counselor may legitimately use it in both ways (pp.231, 233).

Therapy as a means of grace

All therapy can be considered a 'means of grace' as light is shed on the dark side of human spirituality. The Jesuit psychiatrist, W.W. Meissner (1987) advances the thesis that the grace of God is essential to the development and maintenance of a healthy self-identity, both in a psychological and spiritual sense. 'The action of grace must make a difference to the living of the Christian life. It must alter our experience and the course of our life cycle. This does not mean that the action of grace is itself immediately experienced, but it does mean that we are somehow changed and presumably spiritually assisted and advanced by its influence' (p.7). Spiritual identity, suggests Meissner, flows out of the same ego center in the self as personal identity. Where lack of a healthy ego impairs the development of personal identity, spiritual identity will also suffer. Psychoanalytic therapy cannot produce spiritual identity, but the intervention of grace can promote this spiritual development and also assist in the ego's task of personal identity development. This is true because spiritual identity is a function of the ego and thus is directly related to both divine grace and the psyche. Therefore, says Meissner, using 'means of grace' in the therapeutic process will promote both personal and spiritual health. 'Grace is the energizing and relational principle on the spiritual level for the proper functions of the ego. Development of spiritual identity, then, is achieved through the same ego-functions that are involved in the natural psychological identity. The relation between these two levels is based on the operation of the common functions: in terms of psychological identity, these functions operate on their own, but in terms of spiritual identity, there is an added component supplied by grace' (p.58).

Therapy as the empowerment of love

All therapy can be considered an empowering act of love mediated through another person. Love as the motive power for change and growth is a 'means of grace' as presented in the insightful work of the Dutch professor of practical theology Jacob Firet (1986). He presents a threefold process of mediating divine love through the ministry of Word of God. First, a motive power enters the situation in the form of a word or symbolic action; this is understood theologically as the Word and Spirit of God; second, another person acts as intermediary for the release of this motive power; and third, an effect is produced resulting in change and growth. The Spirit of God comes directly to persons as movement on the human spirit, says Firet. The motive power for change and growth does not come from the human spirit alone. Instead, in response to the mediation of love and grace through the presence of another, motive power is induced in the self to move toward health. At the same time, persons who experience this divine grace recognize it as truly a new motive power of their own. (p.101).

The one who enters into this therapeutic relation must do so in such a way that he or she is perceived essentially as a fellow human being, not merely a professional clinician. 'All action toward a human being with a view to his or her humanization has its starting point in dealing with a particular person as a human being... The growth promoter who does not enter the relationship as equal, does not enter the relationship: he not only does not close to the other; he cannot even maintain distance; he is simply not there' (pp.161, 165).

Firet suggests that the mediation of spiritual resources must go beyond, but often include, the proclamation of Word of God (preaching, sermons) and the teaching of truths concerning the Kingdom of God. Persons who hear and understand truth as proclaimed and taught can integrate new ideas and profound truth into their belief system without undergoing transformation and change. He calls this the 'hermeneutic moment,' which occurs when a person says, 'Ah, I understand. I had not seen this before. Now it makes sense to me.'

While this information can change the formal construct of a person's belief system, even about themselves, it does not often lead to change in behavior, argues Firet. There is another movement or moment which must occur for there to be change and this is what he calls the 'agogic moment.'

Through this experience, a person is led to alter behavior patterns and experience new ways of living in conformity to new ways of thinking (pp.99, 133).

The biblical term which Firet uses to define the role of a person who enters into the relation so as to effect this change (agogic moment) is *paraclesis*, a word used in the New Testament to refer to the role of the Spirit of God as promised by Christ. It is a word in the original Greek, often translated as 'comforter,' or 'advocate.' 'And I will ask the Father, and he will give you another Advocate, to be with you forever... I have said these things to you while I am still with you. But the Advocate, the Holy Spirit, whom the Father will send in my name, will teach you everything, and remind you of all that I have said to you' (John 14:16, 25, 26).

A paracletic approach

The growth of the self toward spiritual fitness is not an individual thing. The word *paraclesis* literally means 'one called to the side of another.' To be this person, Firet says, one must go behind the professional role of being a teacher/preacher so as to encounter the other person at a basic human level. As I have made clear earlier, the essential core of each person is spiritual, not religious, so that in being the advocate or comforter (*paraclete*) one can provide a spiritual resource without assuming a religious role. Spiritual resources for mental health and wholeness can be mediated through persons whose own humanity permeates through professional roles so that caregiving involves mutual interchange. In this way one becomes the 'growth promoter' of the other in such a way that both persons experience the effects of divine grace and love.

From this I conclude that in casting light on the dark side of human spirituality we function more effectively and more often as an advocate for the person rather than as an exorcist. Evil isolates, and dark spirituality becomes a tomb of despair. Health and wholeness are more than an individual possession. They are a social and spiritual presence of one to another in the bond of care and community.

This truth is reflected in the valuable contribution made by John Swinton (2000b) when he offers a model of community mental health care based on authentic friendship:

If the church is to be effective in its ministry of friendship, it will be necessary to bring the church and the marginalized together in such a way that both can encounter the humanity of the other and grow together toward mental-health-in-community…the church will have to be *enabled* and *supported* as it struggles to overcome the 'principle of likeness' and to live out the 'principle of grace' within its community. (pp.146–147)

Swinton (2002) suggests that the practicing of virtues 'leads to the development of character that will enable individuals to act according to what is good within their particular encounters. Virtues therefore aim to move a person towards the good, and away from that which is bad or evil.' The particular virtues that Swinton highlights as having therapeutic value are respect, honesty, courage and compassion. These virtues are acquired and practiced, Swinton suggests, in a human community marked by friendship. Friendship, he argues, is an expression of love. 'Friendship is the particular relationship that can be utilized to sit with evil in the hope of reconciliation, one that "treats" loneliness and hopelessness, and deconstructs evil' (Swinton 2002).

The experience of brokenness and the creative power of spirit take place within the life of the body and the care which members have for one another. 'If one member suffers, all suffer with it; if one member is honored, all rejoice together with it' (1 Corinthians 12:26). Spiritual care counters evil with virtue, as Swinton (2002) reminds us. 'When learned and expressed, the virtues are one possible way of countering evil within a clinical context. They enable us not simply to carry out spiritual care that counters evil, but more importantly, they allow us to become the kind of people whose thoughts, actions and influence are so profoundly impacted by love that evil cannot exist in our presence.'

The young woman who came into my office for pastoral care was led into the community of loving and spiritual care. It was in this community, along with some continued psychologically oriented therapy, that she was enabled and empowered to embody the virtues of self-respect, courage, and spiritual faith as components of her healing.

When we experience the dark side of human spirituality within a community of support and care, there is an interchange, a transfusion, if you please, so that what life flows out of us flows back into us, filtered through the fabric of intentional care. Within the life of the self in relation to others, there flows the pain of others as well as the joy of others.

9

The Spiritual Power of Hope in Living with Disability

There is something about the human spirit that defies explanation. We all know people whose spirit refuses to give up, who are moved by some invisible force which gives them a vision of a future giving meaning and purpose for the present.

Alan is such a person. Suffering a spinal cord injury in a motorcycle accident that left him paraplegic, he saw his dream of becoming a professional athlete crash and burn. When suicidal thoughts crept in during the early weeks of his hospitalization, he battled them with a will to live even though he could not grasp either content or purpose. Without a means of making a living, he chose life. Without the means of caring for himself, he accepted care from others as a way of life. Drifting in the twilight zone of an ambiance that excused him from having to lift as much as a finger (literally), he felt the air begin to move his wings (figuratively) and his spirit began to rise.

Having a nodding acquaintance with God through an untested and untroubled childhood faith, he began to respond to the trauma of his paralysis, and directed some pointed questions to the invisible deity that lurked around the edges of his consciousness. 'All right, God,' he said one day, 'You created the world out of nothing, let's see what you can do with me!'

In recounting this, Alan said that for the first time in his life, he viewed God as someone he could talk to without having to be sure of using the right words. 'After all,' he said, 'what more could God do to me? If he didn't like it he could just turn away and leave me alone. I was not in a position to cause him any trouble.'

He received no audible answer, no disembodied voice came to him with the cosmic vibes of a Charlton Heston. Nothing. But a strange stirring in his own spirit took place. 'I felt like part of me had wings,' he said, 'and I was lifted by an invisible breath so that I could see my situation from a different perspective. I gained a vision for what I might do within the limitations of my physical disability, and found a new hope for my life.'

When he was released from the rehabilitation unit and able to use a wheelchair, he enrolled in a program leading to an advanced degree and a professional career. Recently, I asked him a purely theoretical question. 'Alan, if you had a chance to go back and live that tragic moment over again, and escape the accident, retaining your original physical ability, would you chose to do that?'

'That is really hard to answer,' he responded slowly. 'But to do so would annihilate the person that I have now become. I had thought my identity was going to be found through my profession. I have now realized it in a greater sense, being who I am. I have become all that I could have hoped for – what more can one ask of life?'

The spiritual power of hope

That is Alan's story. His soul was moved, I believe, by the Spirit of God and he gained the spiritual power of hope. Early in his life he hoped to find fulfillment and satisfaction through the attainment of a boyhood dream. When he awoke, his life was a nightmare and that hope died. Subsequently, through the brokenness of his spiritual life, and in the agony of his prayers, he had a profound sense of touching the face of God. 'I felt like part of me had wings,' he said, 'and I was lifted by an invisible breath so that I could see my situation from a different perspective.' While his legs remain paralyzed, the wings of his spirit carry him farther than he ever dreamed possible.

The spiritual life of the soul is not a higher form of the self gained by moving beyond the five senses into another realm of consciousness. When Alan spoke of the experience which turned him back into the real world with a new vision of what he could accomplish despite his severe limitations, he used the metaphor of 'wings' and of 'being lifted up' so as to gain a new perspective of his situation.

From his story I learned the meaning of the prophet's poetry: 'Even youths will faint and be weary, and the young will fall exhausted; but those who wait for the Lord shall renew their strength, they shall mount up with wings like eagles, they shall run and not be weary, they shall walk and not faint' (Isaiah 40:30–31).

It is not unusual for persons who suddenly become disabled through injury or illness to question their religious faith and even to demand of God some answer, as did Alan. Unfortunately, theological responses to such questions can result in what Nancy Eiesland (1994) has called a 'disabling theology.' By linking disability to sin, such a theology only serves to further 'disable' a person's coping power and adds an additional burden of guilt and shame. At the same time, Eiesland warns that encouraging the person with a disability to view her or his disability as a pathway to virtuous suffering may not be all that helpful. 'The biblical support of virtuous suffering has been a subtle, but particularly dangerous theology for persons with disabilities... Viewing suffering as means of purification and of gaining spiritual merit not only promotes the link between sin and disability but also implies that those who never experience a "cure" continue to harbor sin in their lives' (pp.72–73). John Hick (1978) revives the theme of the early church theologian, Irenaeus, that this world of suffering is a divinely created sphere of 'soul-making' (pp.318–319). Graham Monteith (1981), living himself with a disability from birth, rejects such a notion when he says, 'The earth seen as a "vale of soul-making" seems to me to be good in intention, but cruel in actual fact. It is difficult to see that any good comes out of disability. It may, in fact, be true, but the disabled, myself included, do not wish to hear it.'

In a more realistic and helpful way, Wendy Farley (1990) says, 'Created perfection is fragile, tragically structured... The potential for suffering and evil lie in the tragic structure of finitude and cannot be overcome without destroying creation' (p.123). She offers a view of divine power mediated through compassion which reaches into our lives, sometimes twisted and distorted by events and forces outside of our control, to empower rather than disempower. This, I believe, is what Alan experienced and what eventually reclaimed for him a view of God that sustained his spiritual life of faith. (For additional sources on approaches to persons with disability see: *Journal of Religion & Disability* 1994; Fine and Asch 1988; Govig

1989; Hillyer 1993; McDaniel *et al.* 1997; Van Dougen-Garrad 1983; Webb-Mitchel 1996; Weinberg 1988.)

The spiritual healing of hope

As it turned out, this was not primarily a religious experience for Alan though it was deeply spiritual. There was no miracle which produced healing at the physical level for which he could credit God. At the same time, he did experience a healing of the soul which resulted in the integration of 'body and soul' as demonstrated in the purpose and mission that empowered him to live and function with his disability. He experienced a spiritual healing of the soul which transformed a disability into a revived ability and allowed him to live normally in a society which is abnormally filled with hatred, pain, and loneliness. His newly discovered spirituality resulted also in a new quality of faith and relationship with God which he considers more authentic and truthful than the simple 'truths' which he professed innocently and naively in earlier years. He discovered the spiritual power of hope to live with his disability.

The psychologist Mary Vander Goot (1987) accurately identifies the source of much unhappiness in contemporary society when she writes: 'Today many people are longing for what now seems like an old-fashioned value, a cause, a goal, or an ideal that could be the lodestar of their lives. The emotional evidence of their predicament is their feeling of fragmentation. Their emotions seem to be like echoes without original sounds. They lack a center: they have no direction' (p.43). There is a hunger which is necessary for us to have faith and to discover hope. Perhaps it is what Jesus meant when he said, 'Blessed are those who hunger and thirst for righteousness, for they will be filled' (Matthew 5:6).

We have all felt it, this longing for fulfillment which lies beyond the horizon of our daily life. Hope is the lodestar that keeps faith on course. Faith is the sail which we raise in hopes of catching a friendly breeze bringing us at last to the safe harbor of our desires and dreams. Without hope, faith is susceptible to the fickle winds of fortune and fate.

While hope must have its center in that which lies beyond the self, its power must be realized and felt in the heart. When we discover the longing which fuels faith and the passion which inspires hope, we begin to experience its power in our lives. A faith which does not arise from this unquenchable hunger for life is not faith but fantasy which can quickly fade. There is a cosmic disposal for beliefs which have lost their value and been discarded. Without the power of hope, faith can lose its own nerve and turn back into despair. We are not born with the passion of hope, but it can be acquired.

The thirst and hunger for hope

Consider the Samaritan woman at the well and her encounter with Jesus. He said to her, 'If you knew the gift of God, and who it is that is saying to you, "Give me a drink," you would have asked him, and he would have given you living water.' The woman protested, 'Sir, you have no bucket, and the well is deep. Where do you get that living water?' Jesus responded, 'Everyone who drinks of this water will be thirsty again, but those who drink of the water that I give them will never be thirsty. The water that I will give will become in them a spring of water gushing up to eternal life.' He thus touched the core of this woman's passion, which hitherto had been indiscriminately poured out in a series of unfulfilling relationships. What others may have seen as promiscuous sexual passion, Jesus diagnosed as an unfulfilled thirst for a love that gave back as much as it took. She cried out, 'Sir, give me this water, so that I may never be thirsty or have to keep coming here to draw water' (John 4:1–15). Practical she was, though a thirst had been opened up in her which would soon become hope and empower her faith.

In his own life, Jesus revealed a consuming hunger for fulfillment which drove him ever deeper into his mission, to go to Jerusalem and present himself as Israel's messiah. When it became clear that this was leading directly to danger, Jesus cried out: 'I have come to bring fire to the earth and how I wish it were already kindled! I have a baptism with which to be baptized, and what stress I am under until it is completed' (Luke 12:49–50). This is passion born out of hope.

The author of the book of Hebrews recognized both the hunger and the hope which Jesus had when he summoned us to look to Jesus, 'the pioneer and perfector of our faith, who for the sake of the joy that was set before him endured the cross, disregarding its shame, and has taken his seat at the right hand of the throne of God' (Hebrews 12:2). Jesus experienced the spiritual power of hope when exposed to the assaults against him. Without the hunger for an ultimate joy he would have chosen a more accessible goal and settled for some form of immediate success. He had plenty of invitations and a score of opportunities to do just that. Without hope as the 'lodestar' of his faith, he would have fallen into the shame of despair and been consumed by the very faith that drove him beyond more attainable goals. Faith without hope can lead to fanaticism and fatalism.

The danger of faith without hope

Mark this well. Faith is a dangerous and destructive drive without hope to sustain its passion. The power of temptation seems to be in ratio to the quantity of faith. One can hardly be tempted if one does not have faith. But having faith as a deeply felt longing for fulfillment in life beyond one's own immediate circumstances means that one can be led astray by the 'fool's gold' which glitters but does not abide. False hope can be the destruction of real faith, as many have discovered to their dismay.

The author of Hebrews writes with pastoral concern, so that those who are awakened to the value of faith may have that faith grounded in a hope that will abide. 'We have this hope, a sure and steadfast anchor of the soul, a hope that enters the inner shrine behind the curtain, where Jesus, a forerunner on our behalf, has entered, having become a high priest forever' (Hebrews 6:19–20). Hope emerges as a spiritual reality when one's self-identity begins to shift from preoccupation with the present tense and moves toward a future tense. Charles Gerkin (1984) includes what he calls 'eschatological identity' as a resource for personal renewal and growth.

> The level of acceptance of eschatological identity is often signaled by a reduction in the self's preoccupation with itself and a concomitant enhancement in the self's capacity for concern for and participation with other persons... Rather than being depleted by the demands and pressures upon the self that threaten the self's existence, the self is increasingly nourished and fulfilled by engagement with others in activities oriented toward the renewal of life together in the spirit of the Kingdom. (p.189)

If faith has its origin in the self's hunger and longing for life's deepest joy, where do we locate hope? For hope to have power in our lives it must also be resident in the feeling self, not merely held in the mind as an abstract concept. If hope is to be a 'steadfast anchor of the soul,' as the author of

Hebrews put it, it must be experienced in the self along with faith. For hope to have spiritual power it must be more than a statement of what one believes. It must be a resident hope, not an alien hope.

The content of hope

To be sure, the *content* of hope lies outside of the self, in God, as the author of Hebrews has testified. It is the content of hope upon which faith finally rests. Without this content, assured by the very reality of God in taking up and giving hope to humanity in its hopelessness, hope shatters like glass under the impact of the 'slings and arrows of outrageous fortune,' as Shakespeare so eloquently put it. But this hope is alien to many people because it does not *abide* in the soul as the counterpart of faith.

As I write this, the morning newspaper tells a tragic story of an 81-year-old man who shot his 78-year-old wife on the patio of their home and then turned the gun on himself as horrified neighbors watched. A friend of the couple reported that the man had recently shared his concern about the evidence of his wife's approaching Alzheimer's disease. 'Who will take care of her if I die?' he worried. On the other hand, others told of their close relationship, their daily walks and journeys to the market as though nothing was wrong. In retrospect, it appears that with no hope for a future the man lacked the vitality of faith necessary to live a life which even in the present time gave them opportunities for enjoyment and shared love. This reveals the close relationship between hope and faith. Without the spiritual power of hope, faith faltered and led to the desperate act of murder and suicide as the only alternative.

Why do so many who claim to have faith lack hope?

THE SPIRITUAL CORE OF HOPE

I believe that the answer is to be found in what we call spirit. Hope arises in the passion of the soul as a longing and hunger for meaning and purpose. But along with passion in the human soul is spirit. Spirit is more elusive than passion, for it exists in the self more as a gift than as a ground of being. In the story of the original creation of the human, we are told that God formed the human from the dust of the ground and 'breathed into his nostrils the breath of life' (Genesis 2:7). The Hebrew word for breath is the same as for spirit. The human self has a unique spiritual capacity which is directly related to the spirit of God. It is spirit in the human soul along with feelings that give rise to hope as a value of the self.

When Jesus appeared to his disciples following his resurrection, we are told that he 'breathed on them and said to them, "Receive the Holy Spirit"' (John 20:22). He thus prepared them to have the assurance of their own shared destiny with him as an indwelling spirit of hope. Peter began his first epistle by reminding us that God, through his great mercy, 'has given us a new birth into a living hope through the resurrection of Jesus Christ from the dead' (1 Peter 1:3). Paul writes that 'hope does not disappoint us, because God's love has been poured into our hearts through the Holy Spirit that has been given to us' (Romans 5:5).

From this we can conclude that hope arises in the human self as God's Spirit moves within us. There is a created human spirit which is given by God through the mystery and miracle of birth, but there is also the Spirit of God which is communicated to the self and experienced as the power of spirit within the self. The Hebrew scholar Abraham Heschel (1962) suggests that, while our passions move us, it is spirit which gives the direction and goal to the self and which empowers hope. 'While spirit includes passion or emotion, it must not be reduced to either. Spirit implies the sense of sharing a supreme super individual power, will or wisdom. In emotion, we are conscious of its being our emotion; in the state of being filled with spirit, we are conscious of joining, sharing or receiving "spirit from above" (Isaiah 32:15). Passion is a movement; spirit is a goal' (pp.96–97).

The source of hope is thus the 'filling of spirit' which empowers the self to release the passion of faith toward the goal which hope sets forth. This is why I define hope as the vision which is seen with the eyes of faith and which satisfies the deepest longing of the heart. This is why genuine feeling, for instance, sorrow or joy, is not possible without spirit. For such feelings arise only out of or in spiritual connections and through spiritual empowerment.

How then do we experience the emergence of hope as spiritual empowerment when the reality which hope grasps in faith so often lies beyond our finite capabilities and our ordinary field of vision? Can we visualize what we cannot see? Is hope based on an illusion?

The visualization of hope

We can only grasp the spiritual reality of hope through some kind of illusion, says Ernest Becker (1973) in his Pulitzer prize winning book, *The Denial of Death*. Life-enhancing illusions, he wrote, are those which arouse faith and produce the character necessary to face adversity with courage and conviction. Such illusions do not lie, but produce authentic faith in the spiritual realities which are true and eternal. By an illusion which does not lie, Becker means a symbol, picture, ritual, or word which promises and points to a reality which is cherished and valued by the self but which cannot be directly grasped. A vow or promise between two people which intends to convey trust and love may be spoken or symbolized in a ritual. While the words can be heard and the symbol observed, the reality to which each points is invisible, but intended to be present and/or promised (pp.199, 202).

The use of visualization to create such illusions is common in the Bible. The Psalmist envisions the blessing of the Lord as a shepherd who guides the sheep to a place where there are 'green pastures and still waters' which restore the soul. 'You prepare a table before me in the presence of my enemies.' The reader is stimulated to imagine the scene and to anticipate the blessing of 'dwelling in the house of the Lord my whole life long' (Psalm 23).

DOES SUCH VISUALIZATION WORK?

The Austrian psychiatrist Viktor Frankl (1963), who was himself a survivor of Auschwitz, in his book *From Death Camp to Existentialism*, reported that those prisoners who visualized life beyond the concentration camp had a higher rate of survival than those who did not. He urged his fellow prisoners to imagine what it would be like to be released, to feast on their favorite food, to walk in the garden, to smell the flowers, and to be embraced by their loved ones. Those who could do this had a higher rate of survival on their meager diet and in brutal conditions.

'I gained a vision for what I might do within the limitations of my physical disability, and found a new hope for my life,' Alan told me in describing the turning point in his life following the accident which left him disabled. The progress he made in rehabilitation in learning to complete small tasks and care for himself even though confined to a wheelchair seemed directly related to the spiritual power of hope which he felt. He continued to visualize himself as functioning in creative and fulfilling ways and was empowered by this hope.

Thomas Moore (1992) suggests that visualization through positive images has a therapeutic effect both psychologically and physically. 'As the traditional medicine of many peoples demonstrates, disease can be treated with images. The patient, for her part, needs to see the images of her healing, just as any of us in distress might look for the stories and images wrapped in our complaints.' For example, says Moore:

> [Robert] Sardello looks at imagery in cancer and concludes that its message is that we live in a world where things have lost their body and therefore their individuality. Our response to this disease could be to abandon the mass culture of plastic reproductions and recover a sensitivity to things of quality and imagination... In Sardello's description of disease, our bodies reflect or participate in the world's body, so that if we harm that outer body, our own bodies will feel the effects. Essentially there is no distinction between the world's body and the human body. (pp.169–170)

Yet, the one who hopes also bears the burden of hope. The description of faith offered by the author of the book of Hebrews implies the visualization of that which is unseen. 'Now faith is the assurance of things hoped for, the conviction of things not seen' (Hebrews 11:1). Hope is the connection between assurance and conviction. It is a vision of a spiritual reality which empowers present faith. By its very nature, hope looks beyond what is seen to what is unseen. This does not mean only what has not yet happened, as only future, but what is present to the person who hopes as a reality assured by faith. 'Hope that is seen is not hope,' the Apostle Paul reminds us. 'But if we hope for what we do not see, we wait for it with patience' (Romans 8:24–25).

The spiritual power of hope produces the capacity to embrace loss and suffer disability without losing faith in life. The Old Testament theologian Walter Brueggemann (1987) reminds us that 'hope emerges among those who publicly articulate and process their grief over their suffering.' Rather than suppressing pain, anger and grief, hope liberates the self to process suffering and losses, transforming them into creative purpose for the reinvestment of self in life (p.84). In other words, the spiritual power of hope is to take up and carry the burden of life, as Alan said, with the 'wings of the spirit.' This is more than poetic metaphor, it is a matter of sowing and reaping.

Bearing the burden of hope

The Hebrew psalmist casts the burden of hope in poetic form:

> May those who sow in tears reap with shouts of joy.
> Those who go out weeping,
> bearing the seed for sowing,
> shall come home with shouts of joy,
> carrying their sheaves.
> (Psalm 126)

A literal translation of the Hebrew reads this way:

> He surely toils along weeping,
> carrying the burden of seed;
> he surely comes in with rejoicing,
> carrying his sheaves.

The burden of hope can only be borne through the practical power of faith. Let me suggest some ways in which faith carries the burden of hope.

THE BURDEN OF ANGUISH

First, the burden of hope is the anguish over what has already been lost. We should never forget this. The burden of hope always emerges out of the ruins of some failed dream, some unfulfilled desire, some loss that must be grieved. In her poignant sonnet titled 'Wine From These Grapes' Edna St Vincent Millay (1956) describes the depressing scene left after the ravaging rage of a flood. The farmer escapes with his life, rowing his boat to safety amidst the ruins and wreckage of his buildings and crops, with a twisted face and a pocket full of seeds (after Millay p.710). He bears the burden of anguish along with the burden of the seed.

If there is a kind of hope that carries no burden, it is childish and immature. An unlined countenance, like that of a child, has not yet learned to carry the burden of hope. Such immature hope is short term and short lived. It flickers brightly for an instant and then just as quickly dissolves with the first tears of frustration over the loss of some simple pleasure.

Hope requires risk, so much that it hurts. Hope makes us vulnerable to fragile plans of future dreams and even greater loss. Hope exposes us to disappointment, frustration, and betrayal. The face of hope may not always be serene and unlined. The loss of one's labor and livelihood, like the loss of the use of one's limbs, is a pain that cuts through to the soul. The countenance of one who hopes bears witness to earlier losses and griefs, but the lines are not unlovely nor permanently disfiguring.

Faith plants the seed and promises a harvest, and so creates hope. But with the promise of a harvest comes the possibility that the promise might also fail. This is the betrayal that hope must bear. Without faith as the investment of one's precious life and resources in the promise of life, the burden of hope could not be borne. But faith bears that burden in partnership with hope, creating our partnership with God, the author and creator of life.

THE BURDEN OF RESPONSIBILITY

Second, the burden of hope is the responsibility that attends the bearer of the seed. The one who bears the seed is not just a container, but a sower! Seed can be borne in a bucket and stowed in a sack. Bearing the seed is to take up the responsibility that lies upon the sower to prepare the soil and to nurture the growth of the seed through to harvest. The burden of hope bears the responsibility for taking up life again when there has been foolishness and failure. This responsibility is not only to sow the seed but also to carry the hope of others whose livelihood depends upon the harvest.

To be a sower one must not only accept the yoke of life and enter into partnership with the creative power of God but also engender the trust of others in the process. In the pocket of the sower are not only the seeds of a future crop but also the hopes of all who depend upon the harvest which is promised.

The gift of faith is God's empowerment to bear the burden of hope and to sow and tend the seed. This seed is an investment of something precious to us in utter dependence upon the promise of a harvest through a power over which we have no control. Our hope, finally, is in God, not in the harvest of our own ambition. When we open the window of hope to the spiritual power of God's love, we find healing for our hurts and hope for our hearts.

The power of the seed is its capacity to draw what it needs from the limitless resources around it, provided that it is sown! This is why the metaphor of sowing is such an apt one for the discovery of hope through faith. Though our faith be as small as a mustard seed, Jesus reminded us, it can move mountains (Matthew 17:20). This is not because of the power which resides in the seed, for it is helpless until it is sown. The power comes from the source upon which faith draws. When our hope is in God, we draw upon his limitless love as the source of our faith.

Empowering hope through a therapeutic alliance of caregiving

On one occasion, in the process of pastoral counseling, I had a person come in for an appointment after many weeks of struggle and exclaim: 'I don't know what has happened. But I awakened this morning and the feeling that I had a weight tied around my neck was gone! I feel free from the burden that we have been trying to get rid of and full of hope and expectation such as I have not had for years.'

To tell the truth, I was as surprised as the person who experienced it! It was not as though I concluded the session a week prior with the knowledge that next week would produce the breakthrough. It was only in retrospect that I could look back and see the signs of recovery which had led to the discovery of a new found sense of peace and wholeness. Discovery has to do with the realization that a transformation has taken place deep within the self (Anderson 1990, pp.67–70).

In my original conversation with Alan in which he recounted the time during his recovery when he spoke of a 'strange stirring in his spirit' leading to the discovery of hope, I asked him if he came to this by himself. 'Not really,' he said. 'A hospital chaplain came to see me every day when I was in the rehab unit. He encouraged me to talk about my anger at God and spent hours with me, over several weeks, allowing me to share my frustration and grieve the loss of my freedom and future. At one point he told me that it was time to take an inventory of my losses. As I listed them he wrote them down on a sheet of paper. It was quite a list! When I had finished he said, "Alan, there is not one thing on this list that you have really lost. You did not mention one thing that you had done or gained in your life prior to your accident that was lost. Everything on your list has to do with imagined losses due to your loss of freedom. But until you have used what little freedom you still have, you cannot lose it." I was shocked to hear that,' Alan told me. 'I still have that paper on which he wrote down what I was grieving as lost. I look at it occasionally to remind myself that grieving for the freedom you have never used is a form of spiritual death.'

The point that Alan made is an important one. He suffered severe limitation and restrictions of movement due to his injury. Others receive distressing news concerning an incurable disease that restricts life to months rather than years. For many, aging often means loss of ability to move about and restrictions which curtail freedoms once thought to be indispensable to happiness. A woman with a severe physical disability once spoke to a group of my students and said that we think of most of you as 'temporary abled,' or 'temps.' We all are going to have to deal with disability in some form, she went on to explain.

Alan was lost in despair over the immense freedom that he viewed as lost. His caregiver insightfully led him to see that you cannot lose the freedom that you have used to create or accomplish something, no matter how small a space that freedom allows you to operate. When he could attach freedom to a task, even to learning to feed himself, he experienced the spiritual power of hope. This is what he described as a 'strange stirring in my spirit.'

THE SPIRITUAL ECOLOGY OF HOPE

I would like to have known the caregiver who entered into Alan's life and helped to instill hope in his life. That person has much to teach us about the spirituality of hope as a vital aspect of effective caregiving. I have attempted in this book to provide a model for what I called spiritual ecology – a spiritual core of the self that integrates 'body and soul,' and empowers the self with freedom to become the self in relation to others and with openness to receive the Spirit of God.

Because hope is dependent on authentic spirituality and because spirituality is grounded in the social construct of being-with-another, the effective caregiver can empower hope where it is weak, gently correct false hope, and plant a seed of hope where hope has died. Alan's caregiver entered into a therapeutic alliance with Alan and has pointed the way for those of us who seek to bring hope to the hopeless.

THE GENERATION OF HOPE

The generation of hope is a slow and painful process of coming to grips with reality – both inside and outside of oneself. The process requires a 'therapeutic alliance' in order to make the therapeutic process the basis of hope. All forms of therapy, says W.W. Meissner (1987), bring relief by raising the level of the patient's morale.

> Hope is, therefore, an act of mutuality, an act of shared imagination, of *imagining with*. To lose hope is to lose the capacity for shared imagination, hope is an act that builds and is sustained by *community*... Hope thus shares in part in the ego's capacity to regress constructively. In so doing, it enables the ego to recapture the sources of imaginative potentiality and creativity. It serves the ego's adaptive purposes by focusing and integrating instinctual derivatives with real possibilities. (pp.195–196, 180–181)

Thomas Moore (1992) argues that the caregiver must enter into the life of the person with an illness in an intimate relation in order to inspire hope.

> As a psychotherapist, if I distance myself defensively from the problems my clients bring to me, I force them to carry universal illness while I try to have power over the disease in order to be protected from it. Healing, however, may ask more from the doctor. It may require a willingness to approach the illness as an intimate, as someone interested in the mystery, and as a member of the human community affected by this disease (p.169)

Strategies for engendering hope

For my own practice of caregiving I have three rules: don't try to give hope; don't take away hope; don't leave a person without hope.

First, it is not usually helpful to try to give hope to a person who is feeling hopeless by attempting to 'cheer them up' with false hope. Too often we are tempted to resort to platitudes in order to avoid dealing directly with the reality of a situation. Alan told me of friends who tried to comfort him by saying 'Nothing has really changed, we will still be friends, we will always be there for you.' The fact was, as Alan well knew, everything had changed and the words of his friends were said as much for their sake as for his. Some offered spiritual hope by talking about the power of God to heal or by trying to convince him that God had a purpose in all of this. 'We know that all things work together for good for those who love God, who are called according to his purpose' (Romans 8:28), he was assured. All such attempts to give him hope only drove him deeper into his hopeless despair. Hope cannot be given by prescription, however well intentioned. It cannot be produced by an act of faith, however one tries. One person cannot give hope to another, it is not contagious.

Second, there are some who take up hope as a defense against the terrible reality and pain which comes with a tragic accident, a devastating diagnosis, or threat to one's life. Christian Beker (1987), professor of biblical theology at Princeton Seminary, tells us that 'When such perceptions of reality become too threatening or are deemed too pessimistic, we create forms of hope which are simply false hope, a result of our unwillingness to see the real world as it is. Thus they are based on the foundation of an illusion.' Such false hope can be deceptive, not only to the person who created it but also to those who attempt to reinforce it as a therapeutic aid. Beker warns that false hope can be as destructive as hopes engendered by a drug trip. 'Hope which is nourished by repression, illusion, blindness, or self-deception becomes false hope. Indeed, expectations and hopes which separate themselves from the realities of suffering in our world become demonic hopes; they cast a spell over us and mesmerize us' (p.21).

False hope is a siren song enticing faith to raise its sails when there is no wind, as many have learned to their sorrow. On many an occasion, when facing the loss of what we value the most, we 'keep our hopes up' that some miraculous intervention will occur and grant us our heart's desire. When our hope is finally crushed by the unavoidable reality of life, the sails of our faith lie tattered and torn at our feet. In the face of the pervasive reality of suffering and grieving life's losses, we face two temptations. One is to give way to the inevitability and apparent certainty of suffering by giving up whatever concept of God sustained us in the past. Frederick Sontag (1970) says, 'Theism tends to atheism when what God accomplishes can also be accomplished without him. If he takes no decisive action in the face of evil, he is not necessary to the process, and someone less pious will soon come along to eliminate God as superfluous' (p.95).

An alternative response is to mask the reality by inventing a coping mechanism of denial, or avoidance, which is really a false hope. Pretending not to see or to feel the evil or pain is a form of self-deception. Temporary relief from the anguish caused by a tragic loss or broken promise by denying present reality and turning to the platitudes and promises of a future hope breaks us off from the real world.

The temptation can be to take away what we know to be false hope in order to force a person to deal with reality. While we know that false hope is a delusion and ultimately destructive to one's faith, we cannot take it away any more than we would snatch a crutch out of the hands of a person who has a broken leg and tell them to walk! No, we leave the crutch of false hope in their hands while seeking to instill hope in their hearts. Earlier in the book I told of Alan who suffered a spinal cord injury that left him paralyzed. He insisted that God was going to heal him and refused the efforts of the caregiver to begin physical rehabilitation. In response, the caregiver said, 'Well, if the miracle does not come today or tomorrow, let us see what can be done until the miracle comes.' In this way, she entered into a therapeutic alliance with him, not taking away his hope of miraculous healing but empowering him to use the limited freedom that he had to perform even a small task.

My third rule is: don't leave a person without hope. This does not mean that hope can be instilled through one encounter. In the case of Alan, the caregiver spent many hours over a period of time and did not end the relationship until hope was inspired. The evidence of hope is not a kind of 'wishful thinking' that everything will change or that something will happen. Rather, it is in the taking up of the 'burden of hope' through attendance to even small tasks that indicates the beginning of hope. In this way, Alan was able to imagine the possibility of taking on larger tasks leading to the completion of a degree and attaining career goals.

Faced with disability or incurable illness, the maintenance of hope as a therapeutic aid for spiritual health is an important dimension of caregiving. The human spirit seeks the recovery of hope even though freedom is restricted and limitations must be accepted.

James Leehan (1989) suggests that the recognition and articulation of imperfection in one's life can lead to hope rather than despair. 'In a special way, survivors are people of hope... Hope is the virtue of those who see the imperfection of the present, who recognize the fear, insecurities, and inequalities that exist, and who work for a new order of things. This

recognition of imperfection and its articulation are critical aspects of hope'
(p. 101).

There is a window of hope in every wall that closes in upon us. There is
a promise of healing for every hurt and a measure of grace poured into
every grief. God has made it so. Hope is not the sun which never sets, but a
morning star in the darkest and longest night.

The inspiration for our faith is poured into our hearts from the
wellspring of hope. The Apostle Paul assures us that 'hope does not
disappoint us, because God's love has been poured into our hearts through
the Holy Spirit that has been given to us' (Romans 5:5).

10

The Human Ecology
of Death and Dying

Upon returning from a period of study abroad, I learned that a member of the church of which I was formerly pastor was dying. As the director of music, she had shared with me a mutual ministry of congregational worship and was a woman of deep spiritual faith. Now, through a terrible and inadvertent consequence of routine surgery, she developed cirrhosis of the liver. She became one of the 'statistically few' who are destroyed through the same medical science which cures. I also discovered that friends who believed that she could be miraculously healed through prayer took her to a healing meeting conducted by a well-known 'faith healer.' When prayers for her healing failed, these friends avoided her and she was left alone to be cared for by her husband as her body slowly weakened. At that time, hospice care was not yet available, and her family was left to cope with her dying. Family members as well as occasional visitors avoided talking about death in fear of causing emotional upset and taking away the hope that she would yet be healed.

At the request of her husband I called on her in the home. As we talked she expressed again her hope that she could be healed and questioned her own lack of faith as the reason why the prayers did not result in healing. At one point, I took her hand and gently asked, 'Has anyone talked with you about the fact that you may be dying?' When she shook her head and said, 'No, not really,' I asked, 'Would you like to talk about it?' Her hand clasped mine with sudden firmness, and she said, 'Yes, I think that it is time. I have known for some time that I am facing death, but no one will talk about it. I guess that they think that they are protecting me and they don't want to take away my hope of being healed.'

Facing the reality of our mortality

Too often, I fear, when we avoid bringing up the topic of death with a person who is dying, we are protecting ourselves from the reality of our own mortality rather than protecting the other person. The 'denial of death,' as Ernest Becker (1975) described it in his book by the same title, can serve as a 'façade of spirituality' draped over the skeleton of the soul entombed behind the audacious pretense of immortality. Out of the fear of our own mortality we 'entomb' persons prematurely in the morbid silence of their own approaching death. Pastoral and professional caregivers must learn to cross the threshold of their own mortality in order to enter the tomb of fear and terror surrounding another's dying and transform it into a sanctuary of spiritual shalom and empowering faith.

As I spoke of death with this woman, I opened two doors: one door to my own mortality which was no stranger to me, the other door to her mortality which, as it turned out, was not the enemy that she feared. As a result she began to face the reality of death as a possible outcome of her situation. She exhibited a depth of emotional and mental composure that indicated a new depth of spiritual peace. 'I have never lost my faith in God,' she said. 'But I bound God to my desperate need to be cured of this terrible thing which is destroying my body. And so God became as alien to me as my own body had become. This is my body, damaged as it is. It is the only one that I have in which to prepare to meet him. I want you to help me to prepare for this meeting.'

The procession from mortality to immortality

A few weeks later, I stood at her graveside, where I spoke of the service as not an end but a beginning. It was a processional, not a recessional. It was a service of committal, but not merely an internment. 'The processional began in her home,' I explained, 'where she experienced the healing power of God's grace and the spiritual reality of her bodily mortality. Now the processional continues, an entrance into life through the hallowed halls of death. We are created and clothed by promise with a spiritual body whose outer surface is mortally wounded. We mortals pause here, in this processional from mortality to immortality. We have accompanied her as far as our mortal bodies can reach, though we stretch out the hands of our faith to make contact with the invisible hands of divine love. Let the processional continue, we shall follow in due time.'

The spiritual reality of our mortality

The spiritual reality of our mortality is the theme of this chapter and points back to the thesis with which this book began. The spiritual core of the human self is the source of ecological wholeness that embraces embodied life as the reality of human life. A spirituality which resides only in the disembodied sphere of the self will fail the embodied self at the most critical point of life, which is death. The spirituality of human mortality is not a 'death-bed' religion, but the core of human life itself. The 'façade of spirituality,' as Becker (1975) puts it, when used to keep death from the door of consciousness, will be exposed as the fraud that it is when the body claims its rightful place in the sanctuary of life.

The human ecology of death and dying

In this chapter I will lay out the contours of a human ecology of death and dying (Anderson 1986, pp.143–159). The human experience of dying is somewhat different than the fact of death itself, as I intend to make clear. Death is not something that occurs after life is lived, but it is part of lived life. Dying belongs to the lived life and is part of it (Moltmann 1985, p.269). Whatever we mean by living in good health, we must remember that the diagnosis for 'good health' is 'mortal illness.' The prognosis for good health is death. The human person is mortally stricken with life (Koestembaum 1976, p.71).

This discussion will be followed by some practical guidelines for caregivers in dealing with dying and death as a spiritual component of human life itself. Paramount in this discussion will be the perspective of practical theology as a basis for caregiving rather than the psychological literature on death and dying. The spiritual nature of human mortality offers unique opportunity for caregivers to approach their task with a view to the human ecology of the social, spiritual, and physical context of living and dying.

Dying as a natural part of living

Theologians disagree as to whether or not human beings were created with mortal or immortal bodies. Those who hold that the original creation of human beings included bodies not subject to dying account for human mortality through the fall from God's grace due to the sin of Adam and Eve (Genesis 3). This was a view promulgated by Augustine (fifth century), affirmed later by Anselm (eleventh century), and taken up by the Protestant Reformers, Luther and Calvin. Some modify this view, holding that the human body was taken from the dust of the ground but endowed with immortality as a divine gift which was subsequently lost in the fall. For example, Millard Erickson (1984) suggests that prior to the fall humanity *could* die; as a consequence of sin humans *would* die. As originally created, human beings possessed *conditional immortality*. 'Given the right conditions,' he says, humans 'could have lived forever.' Just what these conditions might have been he does not explain, except to speculate that before the fall Adam had a body that was susceptible to disease; after the fall there were diseases for him to experience (p.613). The problem with this view is that it tends to explain not only disease but also all aspects of the corruptibility of the human body as due to sin.

Others, including myself, interpret the creation story in Genesis 1 and 2 as intending to suggest that the human bodies of Adam and Eve were mortal and subject to the natural process of decay and death. Modern theologians, such as Paul Tillich (1967), argue that humans were originally mortal beings. The Dutch theologian P.J. van Leeuwen (Berkouwer 1962) argues that 'man as he was created was, and was willed and intended to be, a mortal being. We must deny that death is something unnatural, a break in God's creation' (p.199). Karl Barth (1960a) says that our finite, mortal being belongs to the original nature created by God and not due to sin. The experience of dying is intrinsic to our created human nature (p.632).

THE PROMISE OF IMMORTALITY

The promise of immortality to Adam and Eve was not an endowment of their mortal bodies but something to be realized as a future reality through the power of God to change what is mortal into that which is immortal. 'The first man was from the earth, a man of dust,' says the Apostle Paul. 'Flesh and blood cannot inherit the kingdom of God, nor does the perishable inherit the imperishable...this mortal body must put on immortality' (1 Corinthians 15:47, 50, 53).

In this text the Apostle is contrasting the original, earthly, form of the human body with a new 'spiritual body' which is acquired through resurrection of the entire person, body and soul. The resurrection of the body is not intended to recover an original, immortal body lost in the fall, but is the creation of an entirely new *kind* of body.

WHY IS THIS IMPORTANT?

First, it means that our present mortal body, though subject to the effects of the fall in terms of disease, disability and disintegration, is the bearer of the divine image and the instrument of the human spirit. The creation story explicitly states that 'the Lord God formed man from the dust of the ground, and breathed into his nostrils the breath of life; and the man became a living being' (Genesis 2:7). The Hebrew word for 'breath' is *ruach*, or spirit. The human spirit does not merely reside in the body as in a container, but becomes the life of the body. Our mortal bodies, therefore, weak and fragile though they may be, constitute our spiritual mortality. Our present 'spiritual body' is mortal. The new 'spiritual body' will be immortal. The point of continuity between the two is spirituality, not immortality. The same Spirit of God which breathed the spirit into our mortal bodies will transform our mortality (dying) into immortality (life).

Second, it is important for us to know that our present mortal bodies are the bearers of the divine image and the instrument of our spirituality so that we do not create a 'façade of spirituality' that Becker (1975) warned against with the pretense of immortality. If we live by denying the mortality which inheres in bodily existence we end up treating the body as alien to our spiritual being – something to be despised – or the opposite, preoccupied with preserving the physical body from its inevitable decay and death.

The woman with whom I met was in a crisis of faith and spiritual distress because attempts to heal her body through prayer and divine intervention failed. When she was able to say, 'This is my body, damaged as it is. It is the only one that I have in which to prepare to meet him,' she discovered the spiritual dimension of her mortality. Her body was already telling her that it was dying. When she could accept that, then she could accept that 'I am dying.' She then found spiritual comfort and courage to begin to 'make preparation' for that event, something that her belief system had prepared her for years ago. But it was only when she could integrate mortality into her faith that her faith could grasp the reality and promise of immortality.

BEING HUMAN IS BEING MORTAL

Being human is mortal being, with the promise of immortality. Our bodily existence is itself part of how we experience the reality of life with others in community of being, human relationships and social interaction. Our social being, as the embodied form of our spiritual being, is the concrete form of the image of God. The spiritual being of the self precedes its 'self-identity' as a psychologically conditioned aspect. Theologically, one might say that the image of God as constitutive of the self is more than the religious aspect of the self. It is the entire self, both in its being and its becoming.

I cannot be without or against, but only for, my own body. And my body can only be for me, it cannot live or exist without me. I am embodied soul and ensouled body. Karl Barth (1960a) says, 'We do not have a body here and the soul there, but man himself as soul of his body is subject and object, active and passive – man in the life-act of ruling and serving, as the rational being as which he stands before God and is real as he receives and has the Spirit and is thus grounded, constituted and maintained by God' (p.429). In rejecting all forms of dualism and some forms of monism as abstract, and therefore unbiblical and unhelpful, Barth coins the phrase 'concrete monism' as the only satisfactory concept of the biblical unity of the person as being (not having) both body and soul. 'It is to this concrete monism that we find ourselves guided by the biblical view and the biblical concept of the "soul." The abstract dualism of the Greek and the traditional Christian doctrine, and the equally abstract materialist and spiritualist monism, are from this standpoint a thoroughgoing and interconnected deviation.' What maintains the unity of the body/soul duality of the person, says Barth, is Spirit, that is, the immediate action of God himself 'which grounds, constitutes and maintains man as soul of his body. It is thus the Spirit that unifies him and holds him together as soul and body' (p.393).

Unfortunately, Christian theology has often been tempted to surrender the body to the fate of the dust and pin its hopes on the immortality of the soul. In the fourth century (CE), St Basil of Caesarea (1929) wrote: 'We should not be slaves of the body, except so far as is strictly necessary... In a single word, the body in every part should be despised by everyone who does not care to be buried in its pleasures, as it were in slime; or we ought to cleave to it only in so far as we obtain from its service the pursuit of wisdom, as Plato advises.' But this is to capitulate to an unbiblical way of thinking. The body is not a lower and mortal aspect of the person while the soul is an immortal entity residing in the body as a temporary confinement.

THE MORTALITY OF BOTH SOUL AND BODY

The Old Testament theologian Hans Walter Wolff (1974) says that the soul (*nephesh*) of a person is 'never given the meaning of an indestructible core of being, in contradistinction to the physical life, and even capable of living when cut off from that life' (p.20). The concept of an immortal soul is contrary to the biblical way of thinking. Both body and soul are part of our mortal creaturely being, and both body and soul are to be given immortality in the resurrection (Anderson 1998, pp.175–194; 1982, pp.207–226).

Is death natural?

A distinction can be made between dying as a natural part of being mortal, creaturely being, and death as a judgment of God. The first humans were created from the dust of the ground, placed in the world under God's determination and care, and given a prohibition concerning the tree of the knowledge of good and evil – 'in the day that you eat of it you will die' (Genesis 2:17). For all creatures but the human, dying is itself a natural fate. Human persons are subject to this same fate due to their creaturely nature – from the dust of the ground. That this fate should not come upon them, despite their natural mortality, is due to their life as determined by the sovereign grace and power of God, their creator. When that life-sustaining connection is severed by their disobedience, Adam and Eve now become subject to the fate (death) of all creatures taken from the dust of the ground – 'you are dust, and to the dust you shall return' (Genesis 3:19). Even then, God graciously intervened, providing the promise of life out of death.

WHEN DEATH BECOMES UNNATURAL

Having made this distinction between the natural process of dying and death as divine judgment, what was natural mortality, though suspended by divine grace, now becomes unnatural. Now, says Karl Barth (1960a), 'The death which is behind them is an evil, an enemy of man. In the light of this fact there can be no doubt as to the unnatural and discordant character of death' (p.628). Eberhard Jüngel (1974), however, disagrees with Barth's view of 'natural death.' He feels that Barth's concept of a 'second death' of a spiritual kind is misleading and an unfortunate carryover from the Augustinian tradition. Jüngel fears that this emphasis on a spiritual death rather than a physical death undermines the seriousness of death itself as an event that humans must experience (p.92).

There is no doubt but that it is the evil aspect of death which finally must be redeemed and overcome by God's grace, not merely pardon for sin. The universal human dilemma is not only sin, however it is defined, but death itself, by whatever means it occurs. Because death threatens the very core of self-identity, death attacks the human ecology of the self by severing the body from the soul. This is the inner meaning of the New Testament witness to the resurrection of Jesus from the dead as the basis for the resurrection of the body as the final atonement for sin. The Apostle Paul is emphatic about this with regard to the significance of the resurrection of Jesus Christ from the dead. 'If Christ has not been raised, your faith is futile and you are still in your sins' (1 Corinthians 15:17).

THE INEVITABILITY OF DEATH

The universality of the human experience of death is finally an individual experience which has not changed from the beginning of human history. Philosophers seek to comprehend it with wisdom, poets inspire us to face it with courage, priests clothe it with sacred ritual, psychologists offer inner healing, religion weaves the fabric from which we shape our shroud. Job, the tormented saint, cries out in his agony, 'If mortals die, will they live again?' (Job 14:14).

The question of Job became a classic text in the anguished words of Ivan Ilych, as Leo Tolstoy (1973) tells the story:

> The syllogism he had learnt from Kiezewetter's logic: 'Caius is a man, men are mortal, therefore Caius is mortal,' had always seemed to him correct as

applied to Caius, but certainly not as applied to himself. That Caius – man in the abstract – was mortal, was perfectly correct, but he was not Caius, not an abstract man, but a creature quite, quite separate from all others... 'Caius really was mortal, and it was right for him to die; but for me, little Vanya, Ivan Ilych, with all my thoughts and emotions, it's altogether a different matter. It cannot be that I ought to die. That would be too terrible... It's impossible! But here it is. How is this? How is one to understand it?' (pp.43–44)

BUT WHY ME?

This question 'Why me?' says Helmut Thielicke (1983) 'remains an open one. It remains also an open wound through which faith in the gods threatens to bleed to death' (p.8).

Every culture has its own way of dealing with death. Indeed, says Weisman (1976), every idea about death is a version of life (p.501). At the same time, regardless of how death is understood, interpreted, or faced, it finally remains an undeniable fact. Whether one views death as a Greek, Hindu, Buddhist, Jew, or even as an atheist, death occurs and its result is the end of life as we know it (Anderson 1993b). The typical Western view of death has become more pragmatic and dissociated from religious or philosophical world views. Aging and dying are not seen as integral parts of the life process but as reminders of our limited ability to control nature, despite technological and scientific achievements in this regard. The educated Westerner tends to regard belief in consciousness after death as a manifestation of primitive fears and relics of religion. Nietzsche even went so far as to say that fear of death is a 'European disease,' and attributed it largely to the influence of Christianity (Wolf 1974).

DEFINING DEATH

Despite advances in medical science in the last half of the twentieth century the moment when death occurs is becoming more difficult to define. The empirical sciences explain death in terms of mechanistic and organic processes, with loss of brain function taken as a sign of clinical death. In order to provide the dying with the maximum benefits of scientific medical research and technology, the dying person is usually institutionalized under the assumption that the vital processes of life are essentially organic and physical. Having compartmentalized death so that we no longer live in continuity with the dead, our contemporary culture is none the less preoccupied with an awareness of death such as never before.

The modern hospice movement

An encouraging sign of the development of a human ecology of death and dying is the modern hospice movement. The hospice movement, with a focused care for dying persons, had its beginning with the founding of St Christopher's Hospice in London. Dr Cicely Saunders, founder and director, traces the antecedents of the modern hospice back to the medieval hospices but more recently to Mother Mary Aidenhead, who used the concept of hospice when she founded the Irish Sisters of Charity in the middle of the nineteenth century. Dr Saunder's work at St Christopher's began in 1967, and since that time the hospice movement has developed in England and has spread to the United States (Lattanzi-Licht *et al.* 1998; Shneidman 1976; Stoddard 1978).

At the center of the hospice community is the concept of a body coexisting with a belief. The body is the dying patient, and the belief is that the patient is something more than a body. The hospice community embraces patient, family, and close friends, not only during the final days and weeks of the patient's life but also long after death, offering consolation and support during the time of bereavement.

To summarize this discussion we can say that humanity as originally created by God was not immortal, either actually or conditionally. Human persons, however, as created in the divine image and likeness, were under the summons of God to enter into the gift of immortality to be experienced as transformation of mortal human nature into the immortality which is actually achieved through the resurrection of Jesus from the dead (1 Corinthians 15:35–58).

The spiritual nature of death

Human mortality, even under the effects of natural deterioration and then of sin, is part of the spiritual construct of the human person. Death is not natural and benign, despite attempts to color its dark edges and quiet the voice of terror that rises in the human psyche. Against the psychological and sentimental suggestions to seek the 'good death,' there is something in us that resists the advice to view death as a friend. Death is an enemy of life even though each of us has our own death to die and we need spiritual resources to face this reality.

At the same time, I have argued that human mortality is part of the spiritual core of life itself and we must not allow the dying to sink beneath the surface of our common humanity. A practical theology of death and dying provides a context for the spiritual dimension of caregiving which goes beyond, but may also include, religious beliefs, practices, and rituals. The human ecology of death and dying provides just such a theology for caregiving that preserves the human dignity of life while providing the spiritual empowerment for facing death.

Spiritual caregiving as secular sacrament

The literature on death and dying from a psychological and pastoral care perspective is voluminous and growing. Samuel Southard (1991) provides an annotated bibliography on death and dying. (For other sources see Bregman 1999; Chaban 1998; Cox *et al.* 1992; Kastenbaum 1999; Luchterhand *et al.* 1998; Meyer 1998; Parkes *et al.* 1997; Rosen 1990; Swirsky 1997; Webb 1997; Zurheide 1997.)

The human ecology of living and dying

Practical theology has not yet provided a significant contribution to this area from the perspective of the basic assumptions which underlie the role and practice of the caregiver in approaching persons as whole persons, who are dying or grieving. This chapter, indeed the entire book, has been an attempt to fill this gap by offering a theological paradigm of the human person as an ecological construct of physical, spiritual and social being. The spiritual core of a human ecology of living and dying is grounded in social being, not merely in the self as an individual and separated person.

This opens the door to the entrance of one person into anther's spiritual life without it being an inappropriate 'invasion.' This also means that spirituality is an intrinsic aspect of human life prior to and as the basis for all religious experience and expressions of the self. Because the reality of spirit is first of all a social reality rooted in the nature of human personhood, Dietrich Bonhoeffer (1998) argued, the social structure of human personhood is intrinsically spiritual and prior to all religious formation of the self.

Spirit is necessarily created in community, and the general spirituality of persons is woven into the net of sociality. We will find that all Christian–ethical content as well as all aspects of the human spirit are only real and possible at all through sociality... It will be shown that the whole nature of human spirit [*Geistigkeit*], which necessarily is pre-supposed by the Christian concept of person and has its unifying point in self-consciousness (of which we will also be speaking in this context), is such that it is only conceivable in sociality. (pp.62, 66)

We are spiritual/secular beings

On this basis I suggest that the dichotomy between the religious and secular spheres of human life be eliminated in our praxis of caregiving as a fundamental assumption. Certainly there will be special and specific forms of religious approaches and practices in caregiving depending upon the context and needs of those who need care, especially in the experience of death and dying. However, this does not mean that spirituality itself as a core element of human being should be bracketed off with religion. When this is done it confuses and complicates the practice of caregiving. As the Roman Catholic scientist Teilhard de Chardin (McDonald 1994) has said: 'We are not human beings having a spiritual experience, but spiritual beings having a human experience' (p.76). Persons can thus be considered as spiritual/secular beings who express spirituality and experience it humanly, temporally, and at times religiously.

It is in this sense that I suggest that we view all authentic human caregiving as essentially spiritual (whether or not ostensibly religious) and that the *care* given by the caregiver be considered a *sacrament* in a secular (not primarily religious) sense. Here I must make clear that I am using the term 'sacrament' in the same sense as I have used the term 'spiritual.' If humans are essentially spiritual beings then the mediation of spirituality in the encounter of humans with each other can be considered 'sacramental.' Revelation, as a specific act of God's self-communication to humans 'means sacrament,' says Karl Barth (1957, p.52). By this he meant that for revelation to occur as a form of human experience, knowledge, and benefit, it must come to humans in their own situation and their own context. Thus, Barth (1956b) can say, 'The humanity of Jesus Christ as such is the first sacrament, the foundation of everything that God instituted and used in His revelation... And, as this first sacrament, the humanity of Jesus Christ is at the same time the basic reality and substance of the highest possibility of the creature as such' (p.54).

Spiritual caregiving as secular sacrament

With these assumptions in place, let me now develop further how caregivers can give spiritual care in a sacramental way without intruding religious beliefs and practices into caregiving inappropriately. Further, I want to suggest that entrance into another person's experience of facing death can be done without violating that person's 'space' if it is done spiritually. That is, if it takes place in a way that the caregiver's own spiritual self is open to the other in the encounter.

In a course on Strategies of Pastoral Caregiving, I conducted a seminar with 30 Christian ministers enrolled in a doctoral program representing a wide variety of denominations and religious affiliations. In dealing with the issue of ministry to the terminally ill, I began by asking each participant in the seminar to write out their own obituary, putting down the date of their death, the cause of death, where the death occurred, and who would be present at the graveside service. Out of the 30 members of the seminar, five simply could not complete the task, while a dozen complained that it was not helpful or meaningful to them. They found it too threatening to describe their own death in such concrete and specific ways. These were men and women who had served for at least five years in full-time ministry; all admitted that they had over these years made numerous calls in hospital to persons who were dying and all conducted services for the dead and ministered to the grieving.

OVERCOMING OUR DENIAL OF DEATH

The purpose of this exercise was to confront them with their own 'denial of death' and to help them to open the door to their own mortality as a way of entering authentically into the mortality of others. These were persons who were on the 'front line,' so to speak, of caregiving to the sick and dying. When I probed as to how they dealt with such situations invariably they mentioned the use of Scripture and other religious rituals, including prayer. This was how they were taught, I was told. But I also discovered, as many admitted, that they were using their theological beliefs and religious rituals to arm themselves against their own feelings of inadequacy and even terror at entering into the room of the dying.

The temptation to use theological truth and religious craft as a device to escape the terror of our mortality is especially strong for those who approach caregiving from the stronghold of their religious profession. Dietrich Bonhoeffer (1985), in his lectures to students preparing to enter congregational ministry, said:

> The greatest difficulty for the pastor stems from his theology. He knows all there is to be known about sin and forgiveness. He knows what the faith is and he talks about it so much that he winds up no longer living in faith but in thinking *about* faith... Whoever has once begun to justify himself with the help of theology is in the clutches of Satan. Naturally Satan is a great theologian! But he keeps your understanding three steps removed from your body. (p.68)

Bonhoeffer (1985) himself admitted that it is difficult to speak words of ultimate truth in the context of actual human grief and pain. For the sake of human solidarity and spiritual reality, he confessed to finding himself unable to talk about eternal truths, even though he had these at the tip of his tongue.

> In thoroughly grave situations, for instance when I am with someone who has suffered a bereavement, I often decide to adopt a 'penultimate' attitude...remaining silent as a sign that I share in the bereaved man's helplessness in the face of such a grievous event, not speaking the biblical words of comfort which are, in fact, known to me and available to me. Why am I often unable to open my mouth, when I ought to give expression to the ultimate? And why, instead, do I decide on an expression of thoroughly penultimate human solidarity? (p.126)

SPIRITUAL CAREGIVING AS A SACRAMENT OF 'REAL PRESENCE'

What Bonhoeffer confesses as somewhat of a conflict between speaking the Word of God's truth and being with the person as a form of God's presence, is what I mean by the 'secular sacrament' of 'spiritual caregiving.' One does not always have to remain silent with regard to ultimate truths, nor does one have to avoid religious rituals and practices, such as prayer and Holy Communion. But caregiving as a spiritual encounter must underlie these practices in order to make them effective. And even when they are not deemed appropriate, the sacrament of 'real presence' can still take place.

With the pastors in my seminar, I shared my own experience as a way of explaining what I meant by opening the door to my own mortality in order to enter the door and the space of another's. As I entered the hospital to make a pastoral visit to Colin, who was in the last stages of his terminal illness, I checked my watch in order to see how much time I had to spend with him in order to make my next appointment back in the church office. As I did this, I suddenly realized that I had already decided what I was to say, what Scripture to read, and how to plan my exit strategy. By the time I entered Colin's room I knew that what I needed was not an exit strategy but an entrance strategy. I put myself in Colin's place, watching me enter with Bible in hand, knowing in advance what I was going to do in order to play out my role as his pastor. I cringed inwardly with the awareness that he knew that I was coming as his pastor to fulfill my own responsibility rather than as a friend and fellow human to share in his personal pain and fear.

I had not read Bonhoeffer yet, but I instinctively decided to adopt what he called the 'penultimate' attitude and enter into Colin's life rather than force him to be a spectator at my own performance. After a few minutes of conversation, he confirmed what we both already knew; the diagnosis was deadly and the truth undeniable, he was dying.

'Colin,' I said, after a long pause, 'you know that I am going to walk out of this room and get in my car and drive back to my office. You know that I am going to go home, eat a good meal, and get a good night's sleep. You know that, and there is nothing that I can say or do that will change that. I have a life to live, responsibilities to fulfill, and freedom to do what I please. You know that don't you?'

He looked at me, with a gentleness that I think was meant to convey even sympathy for the awkwardness of my situation. 'Yes, I know that. And I know that I will never walk out of this room and never again do those things.'

It was then that I opened the door. 'Colin, you are doing something that I have never done. You are dying. You are facing the loss of everything that made life meaningful and good. I will have to do that someday. I am not sure I know how to do that. You are doing it well. I am here to learn from you. I need that wisdom. I want you to talk with me about what it is like, what faith and hope is like for you now. Tell me the truth.'

The conversation that followed became the curriculum by which I began to learn what it is to be a spiritual caregiver. I entered the room wondering how much of the 'truth' I would be able to convey to him. Does he know 'the truth' regarding his own situation? Can I tell him the truth? When I was able to say to him, 'Tell me the truth,' the doors opened, mine and his.

The art of spiritual caregiving

Effective caregiving is as much an art as it is a skill. Forrester (2000) says:

> Here the task is more an art, or perhaps a social wisdom (*phronesis*), exercised in close consultation with all involved and with constant honest scrutiny of the practice with a view to its improvement, rather than the application of a theory or a body of established knowledge. It is often based more on a feel for what should be done and accumulated experience constantly reviewed, than upon rules or formal norms. (p.89)

The skills can be acquired through training in psychological techniques and mentoring in the religious craft of pastoral care. The art of caregiving is more a matter of being tuned to the spirit rather than pressing the correct keys on an instrument. 'What human being knows what is truly human except the human spirit that is within?' For the Apostle, this meant that in being a 'sacrament' of care to others, he must 'interpret spiritual things to those who are spiritual' (Corinthians 2:11, 13).

The spiritual reality of our mortality requires a spiritual kind of care. Spiritual caregiving becomes a secular sacrament through which doors are opened. When spiritual doors are open, the Spirit of God breathes once again the gift of life into our mortality. This is the conviction that shapes the life of the soul and forms the substance of faith and hope.

References

Adshead, Gwen (2002) 'Capacities and dispositions: Reflections on good and evil from a forensic psychiatrist.' Royal College of Psychiatrists, Spirituality and Psychiatric Special Interest Group, *Newsletter 7*, London.

Anderson, Ray S. (1982) *On Being Human: Essays in Theological Anthropology.* Grand Rapids: Eerdmans Publishing Company.

Anderson, Ray S. (1986) *Theology, Death and Dying.* Oxford: Basil Blackwell.

Anderson, Ray S. (1990) *Christians Who Counsel – The Vocation of Wholistic Therapy.* Grand Rapids: Zondervan.

Anderson, Ray S. (1993a) 'Anthropology, Christian.' In Alister McGrath (ed) *Encyclopedia of Modern Christian Thought.* Oxford, England: Blackwell Publishers.

Anderson, Ray S. (1993b) 'Death, theology of.' In Alister McGrath (ed) *Encyclopedia of Modern Christian Thought.* Oxford, England: Blackwell Publishers.

Anderson, Ray S. (1995a) *Self-Care: A Theology of Personal Empowerment and Spiritual Healing.* Wheaton: Bridgepoint Books.

Anderson, Ray S. (1995b) 'Self.' In *New Dictionary of Christian Ethics and Pastoral Theology.* Leicester, England: InterVarsity Press.

Anderson, Ray S. (1997) *The Soul of Ministry: Forming Leaders for God's People.* Louisville: Westminster John Knox Press.

Anderson, Ray S. (1998) 'On being human: The spiritual saga of a creaturely soul.' In Warren S. Brown, Nancey Murphy and H. Newton Malony (eds) *Whatever Happened to the Soul? Scientific and Theological Portraits of Human Nature.* Minneapolis: Fortress Press.

Anderson, Ray S. (2001) *The Shape of Practical Theology: Empowering Ministry with Theological Praxis.* Wheaton: InterVarsity Press.

Anderson, Ray S. and Dennis B. Guernsey (1985) *On Being Family – A Social Theology of the Family.* Grand Rapids: Eerdmans.

Aristotle (1987) *The Nichomachean Ethics.* Trans. J.E.C. Welldon. New York: Promethian Books.

Asch, Adrienne and Michelle Fine (1988) 'Introduction: beyond pedestals.' In M. Fine and A. Asch (eds) *Women with Disabilities: Essays In Psychology, Culture and Politics.* Philadelphia: Temple University Press.

Augsburger, David W. (1988) *The Freedom of Forgiveness.* Chicago: Moody Press.

Barth, Karl (1956a) *Church Dogmatics* I/2. Edinburgh: T. & T. Clark.

Barth, Karl (1956b) *Church Dogmatics* IV/1. Edinburgh: T. & T. Clark.

Barth, Karl (1957) *Church Dogmatics* II/1. Edinburgh: T. & T. Clark.

Barth, Karl (1958) *Church Dogmatics* III/1. Edinburgh: T. & T. Clark.

Barth, Karl (1960a) *Church Dogmatics* III/2. Edinburgh: T. & T. Clark.

Barth, Karl (1960b) *Church Dogmatics* III/3. Edinburgh: T. & T. Clark.

Barth, Karl (1961a) *Church Dogmatics* III/4. Edinburgh: T. & T. Clark.

Barth, Karl (1961b) *Church Dogmatics* IV/3. Edinburgh: T. & T. Clark.

Basil, Saint (1929) Loeb Classical Library. *St. Basil Letters.* Volume IV (9). London: W. Heinemann.

Becker, Ernest (1973) *The Denial of Death.* New York: The Macmillan Company, The Free Press.

Becton, Randy (1988) *Does God Care When We Suffer and Will He Do Anything About It?* Grand Rapids: Baker.

Beker, J. Christian (1987) *Suffering and Hope.* Philadelphia: Fortress Press.

Berkouwer, G.C. (1962) *Man the Image of God.* Grand Rapids: Eerdmans Publishing Company.

Bonhoeffer, Dietrich (1965) *Ethics.* New York: Macmillan.

Bonhoeffer, Dietrich (1985) *Spiritual Care.* Philadelphia: Fortress Press.

Bonhoeffer, Dietrich (1998) *Sanctorum Communio: A Theological Study of the Sociology of the Church.* Minneapolis: Fortress Press.

Boyd, Jeffrey H. (1995) 'The soul as seen through evangelical eyes. Part I. Mental health professionals and the "soul".' *Journal of Psychology and Theology 23*, 3, 151–160.

Bregman, Lucy (1999) *Beyond Silence and Denial: Death and Dying Reconsidered.* Louisville: Westminster John Knox Press.

Brueggemann, Walter (1987) *Hope Within History.* Atlanta: John Knox Press.

Brunner, Emil (1979) *Man in Revolt.* Philadelphia: Westminster Press. [1939, London: Lutterworth Press].

Buber, Martin (1979) *I and Thou.* Trans. Walter Kaufman. Edinburgh: T. & T. Clark.

Carson, D.A. (1990) *How Long, O Lord? Reflections on Suffering and Evil.* Grand Rapids: Baker.

Chaban, Michèle (1998) *The Life Work of Dr. Elisabeth Kübler-Ross and its Impact on the Death Awareness Movement.* Lewiston, New York: Edward Mellen Press.

Chandler, Russell (1993) *Understanding the New Age.* Grand Rapids: Zondervan Publishing House (revised and updated edition).

Collins, Kenneth (1995) *Soul Care: Deliverance and Renewal Through the Christian Life.* Wheaton: Victor Books.

Cox, Gerry R. and Ronald J. Fundis (eds) (1992) *Spiritual, Ethical, and Pastoral Aspects of Death and Bereavement.* Amityville, New York: Baywood Publishing Co.

Crabb, Larry (1992) *Real Change is Possible – If You're Willing to Start from the INSIDE OUT.* Colorado Springs: NavPress.

Crosby, Robert C. (1997) *Living Life From the Soul: How a Man Unleashes God's Power from the Inside Out.* Minneapolis: Bethany House Publishers.

Demarest, Bruce (1999) *Satisfy Your Soul: Restoring the Heart of Christian Spirituality.* Colorado Springs: NavPress.

Drane, John (1991) *What is the New Age Saying to the Church.* London: Marshal Pickering (an imprint of HarperCollins Publishers).

Eichrodt, W. (1975) *Theology of the Old Testament, Vol. 2.* Philadelphia: Westminster Press.

Eiesland, Nancy (1994) *The Disabled God: Towards a Liberation Theology of Disability.* Nashville: Abingdon Press.

Erickson, Erik (1950) *Childhood and Society.* New York: W.W. Norton.

Erickson, Erik (1968) *Identity, Youth and Crisis.* New York: W.W. Norton.

Erickson, Erik (1982) *The Life Cycle Completed: A Review.* New York: W.W. Norton.

Erikson, Millard (1984) *Christian Theology, Vol 2.* Grand Rapids: Baker Publishing House.

Farley, Wendy (1990) *Tragic Vision and Divine Compassion: A Contemporary Theodicy.* Louisville, KY: Westminster John Knox.

Fine, Michelle and Adrienne Asch (eds) (1988) *Women with Disabilities: Essays In Psychology, Culture and Politics.* Philadelphia: Temple University Press.

Firet, Jacob (1986) *Dynamics in Pastoring.* Trans. John Vriend from *Het agogisch Moment in het pastoraal Optreden,* Kampen, 1982. Grand Rapids: Eerdmans.

Forrester, Duncan B. (2000) *Truthful Action: Explorations in Practical Theology.* Edinburgh: T. & T. Clark.

Fowler, James (1981) *Stages of Faith.* San Francisco: Harper and Row.

Fox, Matthew (1983) *Original Blessing: A Primer in Creation Spirituality Presented in Four Paths, Twenty-six Themes, and Two Questions.* Santa Fe, NM: Bear & Co.

Fox, Matthew (1988) *The Coming of the Cosmic Christ: The Healing of Mother Earth and the Birth of a Global Renaissance.* San Francisco: Harper and Row.

Frankl, Viktor Emil (1963) *Man's Search for Meaning: An Introduction to Logotherapy.* (A newly revised and enlarged edition of *From Death-Camp to Existentialism.*) Trans. by Ilse Lasch, Preface by Gordon W. Allport. Boston: Beacon Press.

Freud, Sigmund (1961) *The Future of an Illusion.* New York: Norton & Company.

Gallop, George (1997) 'Buddhist practices make inroads in the US.' *The Christian Science Monitor,* November 3, 1997, 9.

Gerkin, Charles V. (1984) *The Living Human Document – Revisioning Pastoral Counseling in a Hermeneutical Mode.* Nashville: Abingdon Press.

Gilligan, Carol (1982) *In a Different Voice: Psychological Theory and Women's Development.* Cambridge: Harvard University Press.

Gorringe, Timothy J. (1999) *Karl Barth: Against Hegemony.* Oxford: Oxford University Press.

Govig, Stewart D. (1989) *Strong at the Broken Places: Persons with Disabilities and the Church.* Louisville: Westminster John Knox Press.

Grant, Robert (1999) *The Orange County Register.* Santa Ana, California, October 14.

Greenwald, Anthony G. (1982) 'Is anyone in charge? Personalysis versus the principle of personal unity.' In *Psychological Perspectives on the Self, 1,* Jerry Suls (ed) Ohio State University, Hillside, NJ and London: Lawrence Erlbaum Associates.

Guelich, Robert A. (1991) 'Spiritual warfare: Jesus, Paul and Peretti.' In *PNEUMA: The Journal of the Society for Pentecostal Studies 13,* 1, Spring.

Hanegraaff, Wouter J. (1996) *New Age Religion and Western Culture: Esotericism in the Mirror of Secular Thought.* Leiden and New York: E.J. Brill.

Hansen, David (1997) *A Little Handbook on Having a Soul.* Downers Grove: InterVarsity Press.

Hauerwas, Stanley (1981) *A Community of Character.* Notre Dame: University of Notre Dame Press.

Hauerwas, Stanley (1990) *Naming the Silences: God, Medicine, and the Problem of Suffering.* Grand Rapids: Eerdmans Publishing Company.

Heelas, Paul (1996) *The New Age Movement: The Celebration of the Self and the Sacralization of Modernity.* Cambridge, MA: Blackwell.

Heschel, Abraham J. (1962) *The Prophet, Vol II.* New York: Harper and Row.

Hick, John (1978) *Evil and the God of Love.* New York: Harper and Row.

Hill, Edmund (1984) *Being Human: A Biblical Perspective.* London: Geoffrey Chapman.

Hillyer, Barbara (1993) *Feminism and Disability.* Norman, OK: University of Oklahoma Press.

Hiltner, Seward (1983) 'Salvation's message about health.' In H. Newton Malony (ed) *Wholeness and Holiness: Readings in the Psychology/Theology of Mental Health.* Grand Rapids: Baker.

Horrobin, Peter (1994) *Healing Through Deliverance.* Chichester, UK: Sovereign World.

Hunsinger, Deborah van Duesen (1995) *Theology and Pastoral Counseling: A New Interdisciplinary Approach.* Grand Rapids: Eerdmans Publishing Company.

Ignatius of Loyola, St (1992) *The Spiritual Exercises of St. Ignatius.* A translation and commentary by George E. Ganss. Chicago: Loyola University Press.

Journal of Religion & Disability & Rehabilitation (1994) Binghamton, NY: Haworth Press.

Jüngel, Eberhard (1974) *Death: The Riddle and the Mystery.* Philadelphia: Westminster Press.

Kaplan, Marty (1996) 'Ambushed by spirituality.' *Time Magazine 147,* 26, June 24.

Kastenbaum, Robert (1999) *The Psychology of Death* (3rd edn). New York: Springer.

Kittay, Eva Feder (1999) *Love's Labour: Essays on Women, Equality and Dependency.* London: Routledge.

Koestembaum, Peter (1976) *Is There an Answer to Death?* Englewood Cliffs, NJ: Prentice-Hall.

Kohlberg, Lawrence (1973) 'Continuities and discontinuities in childhood and adult moral development revisited.' In *Life Span Development Psychology: Research and Theory,* Paul B. Baltes and K. Warner Schaie (eds). New York: Academic.

Kohut, Heinz (1977) *The Restoration of the Self.* Madison: International Universities Press.

Kraft, Charles H. (1992) *Defeating Dark Angels: Breaking Demonic Oppression in the Believer's Life.* Ann Arbor: Vine Books.

Kraus, C. Norman (1987) *Jesus Christ our Lord – Christology From a Disciple's Perspective.* Scottdale, PA: Herald Press.

Lang, Martin (1983) *Acquiring Our Image of God: Emotional Basis for Religious Education.* New York: Paulist Press.

Lattanzi-Licht, Marcia E., John J. Mahoney, and Galen W. Miller (1998) *The Hospice Choice: In Pursuit of a Peaceful Death.* New York: Simon & Schuster.

Leehan, James (1989) *Pastoral Care for Survivors of Family Abuse.* Louisville: Westminster Press.

Loder, James (1989) *The Transforming Moment* (2nd edn). Colorado Springs: Helmers and Howard.

Loder, James (1998) *The Logic of Spirit: Human Development in Theological Perspective.* San Francisco: Jossey-Bass Publishers.

Los Angeles Times, April 21, 2001, A17.

Los Angeles Times, March 16, 2002, A12.

Luchterhand, Charlene and Nancy Murphy (1998) *Helping Adults With Mental Retardation Grieve Death and Loss.* Philadelphia: Accelerated Development.

Lundell, Peter N. (2001) *Armed for Battle: A Balanced Approach to Spiritual Warfare.* Kansas City, MO: Beacon Hill Press of Kansas City.

McDaniel, Susan H., Jen Hepworth, and William Doherty (eds) (1997) *The Shared Experience of Illness: Stories of Patients, Families & Their Therapists.* New York: Basic Books.

McDonald, Gordon (1994) *The Life God Blesses.* Nashville: Thomas Nelson Publishers.

McFadyen, A.I. (1990) *The Call to Personhood – A Christian Theory of the Individual in Social Relationships.* Cambridge and New York: Cambridge University Press.

McGill, Arthur C. (1982) *Suffering: A Test of Theological Method.* Philadelphia: Westminster.

Macmurray, John (1935) *Reason and Emotion.* London: Faber & Faber.

Macmurray, John (1961) *Persons in Relation.* London: Faber & Faber.

McRoberts, Kerry D. (1989) *New Age or Old Lie?* Peabody, MA: Hendrickson Publishers.

Malony, H. Newton (ed) (1983) *Wholeness and Holiness: Readings in the Psychology/Theology of Mental Health.* Grand Rapids: Baker.

Means, Jeffrey J. (2000) *Trauma & Evil: Healing the Wounded Soul.* Minneapolis: Fortress Press.

Meissner, W.W. (1987) *Life and Faith: Psychological Perspectives on Religious Experience.* Washington, DC: Georgetown University Press.

Melton, J. Gordon, Jerome Clark and Aidan A. Kelly (1990) *New Age Encyclopedia: A Guide to the Beliefs, Concepts, Terms, People, and Organizations that Make up the New Global Movement Toward Spiritual Development, Health and Healing, Higher Consciousness, and Related Subjects* (1st edn). Detroit, MI: Gale Research.

Merton, Thomas (1960) *The Wisdom of the Desert.* New York: New Directions Books.

Meyer, Charles (1998) *A Good Death: Challenges, Choices, and Care Options.* Mystic, CT: Twenty-Third Publications.

Millay, Edna St Vincent (1956) 'Wine from these grapes' (sonnet 10). In *Collected Poems,* Norman Millay (ed). New York: Harper and Row.

Miller, Keith (1996) *Taste of New Wine.* Waco, TX: Word Books.

Miller, Keith (1997) *The Secret Life of the Soul.* Nashville: Broadman and Holman, Publishers.

Moltmann, Jürgen (1974) *The Crucified God.* London: SCM Press.

Moltmann, Jürgen (1985) *God in Creation: A New Theology of Creation and the Spirit of God.* San Francisco: Harper and Row.

Monteith, W. Graham (1981) 'Too many awkward questions – too many glib answers.' In *University of Edinburgh Bulletin,* Edinburgh, Scotland.

Moore, Thomas (1992) *Care of the Soul: A Guide for Cultivating Depth and Sacredness in Everyday Life.* New York: HarperCollins.

Moseley, Romney (1991) *Becoming a Self – Critical Transformations Before God.* Nashville: Abingdon Press.

Oden, Thomas (1987) *The Living God: Systematic Theology (vol. I).* San Francisco: Harper and Row.

O'Neill, Eugene (1982) 'The great god brown.' *The Plays of Eugene O'Neill (vol. 1).* New York: Modern Library.

Orange County Register (2001) Santa Ana, California. Friday, September 21, p.30.

Oropeza, B.J. (1997) *99 Answers to Questions About Angels, Demons & Spiritual Warfare.* Downers Grove: InterVarsity Press.

Otis, George (1997) *The Twilight Labyrinth: Why Does Spiritual Darkness Linger Where it Does?* Grand Rapids: Chosen Books.

Pannenberg, Wolfhart (1985) *Anthropology in Theological Perspective.* Philadelphia: Westminster Press.

Parkes, Colin Murray, Pittu Laungani, and Bill Young (eds) (1997) *Death and Bereavement Across Cultures.* London and New York: Routledge.

Peck, S. Scott (1997) *Denial of the Soul: Spiritual and Medical Perspectives on Euthanasia and Mortality.* New York: Harmony Books.

Perls, Frederick (Fritz) and Laura Perls (1976) *The Gestalt Approach and Eye Witness to Therapy*. New York: Bantam Books.

Piaget, Jean (1967) *Six Psychological Studies*. New York: Random House, Vintage Books.

Pieper, Josef (1969) *Death and Immortality*. New York: Herder and Herder.

Pinnock, Clark H. (2001) *Most Moved Mover: A Theology of God's Openness*. Grand Rapids: Baker.

Rhodes, Ron (1995) *The New Age Movement*. Grand Rapids: Zondervan.

Rosen, Elliott J. (1990) *Families Facing Death: Family Dynamics of Terminal Illness*. Lexington, MA: Lexington Books.

Saucy, Robert L. (1993) 'Theology of human nature.' In J.P. Moreland and David M. Ciocchi (eds) *Christian Perspectives on Being Human: A Multidisciplinary Approach to Integration*. Grand Rapids: Baker.

Scarry, Elaine (1985) *The Body in Pain: The Making and Unmaking of the World*. New York: Oxford University Press.

Shneidman, Edwin S. (ed) (1976) *Death: Current Perspectives*. Palo Alto, CA: Mayfield Publishing.

Shuster, Marguerite (1987) *Power, Pathology and Paradox: The Dynamics of Evil and Good*. Grand Rapids: Zondervan.

Smedes, Lewis B. (1984) *Forgive and Forget: Healing the Hurts We Don't Deserve*. San Francisco: Harper and Row.

Sontag, Frederick (1970) *The God of Evil*. San Francisco: Harper and Row.

Southard, Samuel (1989) *Theology and Therapy*. Dallas: Word.

Southard, Samuel (1991) *Death and Dying: A Bibliographical Survey*. New York: Greenwood Press.

Stoddard, Sandol (1978) *The Hospice Movement: A Better Way of Caring for the Dying*. Briar Cliff Manor, New York: Stein and Day.

Swinton, John (2000a) *Toward a Practical Theology of Human Nature, Interpersonal Relationships, and Mental Health Care*. New York: Peter Lang.

Swinton, John (2000b) *Resurrecting the Person: Friendship and the Care of People with Mental Health Problems*. Nashville: Abingdon Press.

Swinton, John (2002) 'Does evil have to exist to be real? The discourse of evil and the practice of mental health care.' Royal College of Psychiatrists Spirituality and Psychiatric Special Interest Group. *Newsletter 7*, London.

Swirsky, Michael (ed) (1997) *At the Threshold: Jewish Meditations on Death*. Northvale, NJ: J. Aronson.

Teresa of Avila (1961) *The Interior Castle*. New York, NY: Bantam, Dell & Doubleday, Inc.

Thomas, Dylan (1971) *The Poems of Dylan Thomas*. New York: New Directions Publications.

Thomas, John C. (1998) *The Devil, Disease and Deliverance: Origins of Illness in New Testament Thought.* Sheffield, UK: Sheffield Academic Press.

Thomas à Kempis (1952) *The Imitation of Christ.* Bergenfield, NJ: Viking-Penguin Inc.

Thielicke, Helmut (1983) *Living With Death.* Grand Rapids: Eerdmans Publishing Company.

Tillich, Paul (1967) *Systematic Theology (vol 2).* Chicago: University of Chicago Press.

Timmer, John (1988) *God of Weakness.* Grand Rapids: Zondervan.

Tolstoy, Leo (1973) *The Death of Ivan Ilych.* New York: Health Sciences Publishing.

Torrance, Thomas F. (1981) *Divine and Contingent Order.* Oxford: Oxford University Press.

Towner, W. Sibley (1976) *How God Deals with Evil.* Philadelphia: Westminster Press.

Trible, Phyllis (1978) *God and the Rhetoric of Sexuality.* Philadelphia: Fortress.

Ulanov, Ann and Barry Ulanov (1982) *Primary Speech: A Psychology of Prayer.* Atlanta: John Knox Press.

Vander Goot, Mary (1987) *Healthy Emotions: Helping Children Grow.* Grand Rapids: Baker.

Van Dougen-Garrad, Jessie (1983) *Invisible Barriers: Pastoral Care with Physically Disabled People.* London: SPCK.

von Balthasar, Hans Urs (1967) *A Theological Anthropology.* New York: Sheed and Ward.

Wagner, C. Peter (1992) *Warfare Prayer: How to Seek God's Power and Protection in the Battle to Build His Kingdom.* Ventura, CA: Regal Books.

Wagner, C. Peter (1993) *Breaking the Strongholds in Your City.* Ventura, CA: Regal Books.

Walker, Dominic (2002) 'Is evil necessary?' Royal College of Psychiatrists. Spirituality and Psychiatric Special Interest Group, *Newsletter 7*, London.

Wallis, Claudia (1996) 'Faith and healing.' In *TIME Magazine 147*, 26, June 24, 1996. Reported by Jeanne McDowell/Los Angeles, Alice Park/New York and Lisa H. Towle/Raleigh.

Walsh, James and P.G. Walsh (1985) *Divine Providence and Human Suffering: Message of the Fathers of the Church.* Wilmington, DE: Michael Glazer.

Webb, Marilyn (1997) *The Good Death: The New American Search to Reshape the End of Life.* New York: Bantam Books.

Webb-Mitchell, Brett (1996) *Dancing with Disabilities: Opening the Church to All God's Children.* Cleveland, OH: United Church Press.

Webster, Douglas D. (1999) *Soulcraft: How God Shapes us Through Relationships.* Downers Grove: InterVarsity.

Weinberg, N. (1988) 'Another perspective: attitudes of people with disabilities.' In H.E. Yuker (ed) *Attitudes Toward Persons with Disabilities*, pp.141–153. New York: Springer.

Weisman, Avery D. (1976) 'Appropriate and appropriated death.' In Edwin S. Shneidman (ed) *Death: Current Perspectives*. Palo Alto, CA: Mayfield Publishing.

Wicker, Allan (1979) *Introduction to Ecological Psychology*. Monterey, CA: Brooks-Cole Publishing Company.

Will, James (1989) *A Christology of Peace*. Louisville: Westminster John Knox Press.

Wink, Walter (1986) *Unmasking the Powers: The Invisible Forces that Determine Human Existence*. Philadelphia: Fortress Press.

Wink, Walter (1992) *Engaging the Powers: Discernment and Resistance in a World of Domination*. Minneapolis: Fortress Press.

Wink, Walter (1998) *The Powers that Be: Theology for a New Millennium*. New York: Doubleday.

Wolf, Richard (1974) *The Last Enemy*. Washington, DC: The Canon Press.

Wolff, Hans Walter (1974) *Anthropology of the Old Testament*. Philadelphia: Fortress Press.

Wynne, Lyman C., Susan H. McDaniel, and Timothy T. Weber (eds) (1986) *Systems Consultation: A New Perspective for Family Therapy*. New York: Guilford Press.

Zukav, Gary (1989) *The Seat of the Soul*. New York: Simon & Schuster.

Zukav, Gary (1994) *Thoughts from the Seat of the Soul: Meditations for Souls in Process*. New York: Simon & Schuster.

Zurheide, Jeffrey R. (1997) *When Faith is Tested: Pastoral Responses to Suffering and Tragic Death*. Minneapolis: Fortress Press.

Subject Index

Author Index

4826046

Made in the USA
Lexington, KY
05 March 2010